P R

The Carry-On Imperative

"In Robin's unique style, she recounts a powerfully poignant story of life-shaping, traumatic losses in her early years. Yet she does not let these losses rule her life, making this also a story of resilience, hope, and healing. You will cry and laugh—maybe at the same time—as you read. Robin's honesty invites all of us to realize we are not alone."

—**RUTH VAN REKEN**, co-author,
Third Culture Kids: Growing Up Among Worlds

"Reading Robin's memoir is like sitting down for a drink with your favourite sister and getting her to dish all her favourite stories. It's sharply observed and funny, and is a fast, breezy read about someone claiming her own identity and history across multiple continents and cultures. I came away with a sense of someone who, through telling her story, has found her roots, and is generous enough to share that journey with us."

—**KAILE SHILLING**, executive director, Vancouver Writers Fest

"An inspiring story of one woman's journey learning the skill of transitioning through cultures, life phases, and multiple reinventions. Capped with the perfect tale of 'late work': a purpose-driven duet with her partner that scales the world. A message for our time: Grow and give. And never stop."

—**AVIVAH WITTENBERG-COX**, host, *4-Quarter Lives* podcast

"With refreshing honesty, Robin's voice comes across strong as she weaves a story of loss, learning, and living. Her stories and many of her reflections will resonate with those who live globally mobile lives."

—**HANNELE SECCHIA**, president, Families in Global Transition

"This is a great memoir that Third Culture Kids and their parents won't be able to put down. It speaks our language. In the years I have known and worked with Robin, she has consistently modelled her values and not wavered from the hard work to pursue her dreams. Even though I think I may know all about the international lifestyle, I always learn so much from her books and this one is no exception!"

—LOIS J. BUSHONG, Third Culture Kid, counsellor, and author of *Belonging Everywhere and Nowhere: Insights into Counseling the Globally Mobile*

"Robin Pascoe's entertaining and internationally focused memoir aptly reflects her reverence and passion for resilience. Whether dealing head-on with circumstances beyond her control, embracing waves of unremitting change requiring near-continuous reinvention, striving to maintain emotional equilibrium and a healthy sense of self, or continually seeking the positive and the pragmatic, Pascoe models a lifelong insistence on meaning and contribution."

—LINDA A. JANSSEN, author of *The Emotionally Resilient Expat*

"There is a relentless, resilient, don't-take-no-for-an-answer quality that comes beaming through Robin's stories in *The Carry-On Imperative*. Great if you happen to be a journalist, even better if you're trying to build a life as an itinerant author, mother, partner, speaker. If I had to describe Robin based solely on the stories here, without ever having met her, it would be 'Carpe fucking diem!' "

—DAVID DOWNEY, friend and colleague at CBC Winnipeg

"This is a touching story about a young, vulnerable girl who experienced unimaginable grief; a wife who saw her struggles reflected in others and did something about it; and a philanthropist who set out to repair the world. Thank you, Robin, for sharing yourself so freely, for giving us all permission to cope by any means necessary, and for continuing to make the world a better place. And of course, thank you, Auntie Goldie."

—**JULIA STAUB-FRENCH,** executive director,
Family Services of the North Shore, North Vancouver, BC

"Robin's inspirational story epitomizes overcoming immense losses and personal challenges to build a successful life and ultimately contributing toward positive change in the world through her philanthropy. . . . Lions Gate Hospital Foundation and the social, health, and environmental causes that have benefited from Robin's generosity can thank her auntie Goldie for instilling the value of giving back."

—**JUDY SAVAGE,** president and CEO, Lions Gate Hospital Foundation

ALSO BY ROBIN PASCOE

A Broad Abroad
The Expat Wife's Guide to Successful Living Abroad

Culture Shock
A Parent's Guide

Homeward Bound
A Spouse's Guide to Repatriation

A Moveable Marriage
Relocate Your Relationship without Breaking It

Raising Global Nomads
Parenting Abroad in an On-Demand World

THE CARRY-ON IMPERATIVE

The Carry-On Imperative

A MEMOIR OF TRAVEL, REINVENTION & GIVING BACK

ROBIN PASCOE

Botania Books

Botania Books

North Vancouver, British Columbia, Canada
www.robinpascoe.com

Editing by Barbara Pulling

Copy-editing and proofreading by
Naomi Pauls, Paper Trail Publishing

Cover and text design by Jan Perrier, Perrier Design

Publisher's Cataloguing-in-Publication data

Names: Pascoe, Robin (Journalist), author.

Title: The carry-on imperative : a memoir of travel, reinvention, and giving back / Robin Pascoe.

Description: North Vancouver, BC: Botania Books, 2023.

Identifiers: ISBN: 978-1-7389040-0-6 (paperback) | 978-1-7389040-2-0 (Kindle) | 978-1-7389040-3-7 (e-book)

Subjects: LCSH Pascoe, Robin. | Pascoe, Robin—Travel. | Travel writers—Biography. | Asia—Travel. | Voyages and travels. | BISAC BIOGRAPHY & AUTOBIOGRAPHY / Editors, Journalists, Publishers | BIOGRAPHY & AUTOBIOGRAPHY / Personal Memoirs | BIOGRAPHY & AUTOBIOGRAPHY / Women | TRAVEL / Asia / General | TRAVEL / Essays & Travelogues

Classification: LCC G154.5.P37 2023 | DDC 910.4/092—dc23

For Lucy Rose

Contents

THE CARRY-ON IMPERATIVE

Setting the Stage

I HAD NEVER written anything longer than a book report for school when I created a one-act play at summer camp. It was my team's entry for the drama competition in Camp Kadimah's annual Olympic games, known as Maccabia. The year was 1967, and I was fourteen. I suspected that my team captains, two counsellors not much older than I was, felt sorry for the motherless waif with the bad haircut. *Poor Robin*, I imagined them saying to one another. *She's had such a rough time. Let her write our team play.* Normally, I couldn't tolerate being singled out and would run a mile to avoid anyone's pity. I just wanted to fit in, without a spotlight shining on me—even a kind and compassionate one. But for some compelling reason, I needed to write this play.

I was really having a run of bad luck. Eighteen months earlier, my mother had died during a lengthy surgery to repair a brain aneurysm that had come out of nowhere, like they always do. I was so distracted with grief when I returned to school, I tripped in my gym class, badly injuring my foot. In front of the whole school, the principal, Mr. Wall, carried me out to his car before driving me home. What I remember most, besides the humiliating spectacle of crying in front of my classmates, was that he reeked of cigarettes. I found the smell oddly comforting. My mother had smoked a lot. It was as if she were hovering nearby. My bereaved father, meanwhile, had just returned to his dental office after getting up from the family's *shiva*, our week of mourning. When the school called him, he cancelled all his patients and came racing home. Exhausted and shaken, he took me for an X-ray.

Broken. My foot and my family.

For six long weeks, I was a lonely figure eating lunch in my classroom without anyone to keep me company, a heavy plaster cast on my foot and crutches close at hand. It was an age when children went home for their midday meal, but there was no one to pick me up. Teachers walking by the classroom would poke their heads in to say hello, to ask me if I needed anything, and to say how sorry they had been to hear about my mom. Their discomfort in speaking about her death was obvious. And who could blame them for looking away? I was small for my age and looked a lot younger than twelve. All anyone could see was a very sad and lonely little girl. I allowed my self-pity to give me permission to snoop around my classmates' desks and found notes exchanged by my two best friends.

"Can you believe all the attention she's getting?" one friend wrote to the other.

"I know! And don't you think she's feeling awfully sorry for herself?" the other friend asked.

You bet I was. No one at my elementary school had ever had their mother die before. Or broken their foot. All in the space of just one week. *Poor Robin.*

• • •

Pop culture remembers 1967 as the Summer of Love. It was also the year of the Six-Day War in the Middle East. The shocking, rapid-fire Israeli victory over the armies of the Arab world was all anyone could talk about at my summer camp, especially since the camp was run by a Zionist youth organization. On that topic, I had a story worthy of dramatization, inspired by the experience of my cousin David from Toronto. He was living on a kibbutz in Israel when the war broke out. Along with many other young men from the Jewish diaspora, David felt the urge to help out in the fight. But the idea of volunteering had prompted much intellectual and cultural soul-searching from the pulpits of synagogues and in the mainstream press on questions of national allegiance and identity.

On the makeshift stage in the camp rec hall, where a year earlier I had played the daughter who marries a *goy* in *Fiddler on the Roof*, a young man pondered whether or not to go to Israel to fight. "Am I a Jewish Canadian? Or a Canadian Jew?" he (played by me) wondered. *Who am I? Where do I belong?* These were questions top of mind for a girl whose connection with the woman who gave her life had been severed without warning.

Writing and acting in that play released emotions that had been strangling me. I was able to breathe again for the first time in months. Our play won the drama competition but that was beside the point. After we took our bows, my camp friends surrounded me with hugs that were not just for my performance. I didn't know it at the time, but I had stumbled upon a way to connect to my grief that would guide me for the rest of my life.

ONE

Channelling
Mary Tyler Moore

PEOPLE ENVY ME for the easy way I communicate with others, even with someone I'm meeting for the first time. From the briefest of encounters, often with just my smile, I can take away amazing nuggets of personal information. It's true, I can be overly loquacious. Family and friends will agree, though, that I'm a good listener too. Being empathetic helps. "I'm not sure why I'm even telling you this story, Robin. I've never told anyone before." Intimate secrets are only shared with good listeners. And journalists, of course. Given my natural ability to collect other people's stories, no one was surprised when I decided to become a reporter.

Like my peer group of wannabe reporters back in the 1970s, I idolized and was inspired by Bob Woodward and Carl Bernstein of the *Washington Post*. The intrepid scribes of the Watergate scandal lifted the profile of the profession significantly when they brought down Richard Nixon. But it was *The Mary Tyler Moore Show* that made a greater impact on me.

Mary Richards and the gang in her Minneapolis television newsroom WJM, especially anchorman Ted Baxter and news director Lou Grant, were pop culture's shining avatars of broadcast journalism. Mary's character represented harmless, innocuous feminism, a woman *making it after all* while looking absolutely gorgeous. Mary throwing her hat into the air at the end of the famous opening credits was television's benign version of the battle cry for young women of my generation to strike out on their own. That was certainly my plan.

I entered journalism school in the fall of 1975. The night before I left home, my family took me out for dinner at Lichee Garden in the heart of Toronto's Old Chinatown. For baby boomers growing up in Toronto, Lichee Garden was the go-to destination for special occasions. For Jewish families, it was the choice on any given Sunday night. We gorged on what we considered tasty Chinese delicacies, including my personal favourite, pork ends. I would later discover this was a Canadianized dish and not served anywhere in China.

Just as my family was finishing up our very non-kosher banquet of pork and shrimp, my father decided to say a few words. Rising from his seat, drink in hand (Lichee Garden was only the second restaurant in then puritanical Toronto to secure a liquor license), he toasted my acceptance into the highly competitive graduate journalism program at Carleton University in Ottawa. He was being very sweet, but he should have stopped speaking sooner.

"Journalism will be a wonderful second career for you, Rob," my father pronounced.

I almost choked on my egg roll, spitting it out along with my rejoinder. "So what's my *first* career, Dad?"

His answer came without a moment's hesitation. "Being a wife and mother, of course."

"I haven't even started journalism school and already you have me abandoning the profession for a man. I'm not a stereotype,

Dad. In fact, this is exactly how they keep being perpetuated! By men like you."

"There's no need to turn this into one of your feminist arguments, *Ms.* Pascoe," my father said in exasperation, deliberately emphasizing the new honorific that I had acquired along with a subscription to *Ms.* magazine. As it turned out, the iconic feminist publication would print my very first magazine article less than a decade after this dinner. The piece was about the rights of Indigenous women at the time of the repatriation of Canada's constitution from Great Britain.

But on that night, my father simply wanted to make his point. "As a journalist, Rob, you'll have the option of freelancing from home. You can continue working while looking after your family. One day you're going to appreciate that."

Like his given name, which was Herb, my father was an old-fashioned fellow, an affable, good-looking man despite a nose that had been broken during his days playing hockey as a teenager on the Saskatchewan prairie. Herb loved to wear stylish hats, drink Manhattans, watch golf on television right after playing a round of it, and hit the racetrack on the weekends. On weekdays, he was Dr. Pascoe, a dentist on Toronto's Danforth Avenue.

His tone that long-ago evening contained the weariness he shared with other fathers of his era. Like his cohort, men who came of age during the Second World War, Herb was trying to raise a daughter hell-bent on burning her bra (metaphorically, as I didn't even need one back then). He had endured hours of me lecturing on the wisdom of Gloria Steinem and other second-wave feminists.

"I won't be working from home!" went my passionate come-back that night. "I'll be working in a newsroom. If I happen to marry and have children, and who says I even *have* to marry, my kids will definitely be put into daycare." I spoke with all the outrage, conviction, and certainty of a twenty-two-year-old woman who had barely begun to live her life.

• • •

There were many eager young crusaders in the seventies, leading to stiff competition for places in journalism schools. For me, capturing a coveted spot at Carleton was the result of a year's worth of plotting.

It was 1974 and I had just finished my undergraduate degree at Dalhousie University on the east coast of Canada—one of four institutions of higher learning in Halifax. With so many students my age in town, unsurprisingly, my major in English literature was accompanied by a minor in serious partying (and drinking bad coffee all day at the Student Union Building). Upon gradu-ation, I realized my degree wasn't going to move me any closer to gainful employment without more education and training. Many of my friends began applying to graduate school, with law school being particularly popular. Instead, I decided to search for a job to generate sample news clippings for my application to journalism school.

I caught two early breaks. First, I persuaded the manager at the local office of a national public relations company to hire me for an entry-level job. When that seemed to be working out, the manager arranged to share my time with a good friend of his who had launched a community newspaper in a suburb outside of

Halifax. As my boss saw it, reporting would enhance the writing skills I could bring to the PR firm. It was a creative win-win scenario and my second lucky break.

For the next year, I worked both jobs: learning the communications ropes at the PR firm two days a week and serving as the first reporter for the *Bedford-Sackville News* on the other three. Given that foundational template, it's no wonder I would go on to spend almost fifty years straddling the worlds of journalism and corporate communications.

The *B-S News*, as I cheekily referred to the weekly broadsheet, became my own version of a five-thousand-watt radio station in the middle of nowhere. Like Ted Baxter, I'd be able to claim I got my start in the sticks. I started from scratch at the paper, having never written a news story before. Socializing had kept me too busy to work on the university newspaper at Dal. But I had a remarkable tutor in the paper's founder, David Bentley. David was a British journalist who would become infamous in Canadian journalism circles fifteen years later for publishing *Frank* magazine, a national scandal sheet modelled after Fleet Street's gossip tabloids. Fleet Street was where David had got his own start, and *Frank*'s Ottawa edition was notorious for ripping apart Canadian media personalities and politicians.

My first newsroom was my mentor's kitchen. David and his wife, Diana, had bought townhouses side by side with another British couple in Lower Sackville, up the road from Bedford, and together they published the weekly from their homes. I still felt like a reporter, even though I had to bring my own typewriter to work and chat politely with a toddler before turning to current events with my editor, his father.

David Bentley was the ideal teacher for someone just starting out. A tall, thin bloke with a receding hairline and nervous
energy to burn, he tolerated no excuses on any matter. Had I
screwed up and not asked hard questions of someone I was inter-
viewing? "Get on the phone and call back. Go back in person
if necessary. Now!" Had I complained about having to use a
typewriter, in the days before keyboards were extensions of our
fingers? "Get over it! Reporters write on typewriters, not with
a pen." Did I know how to use a camera? he asked. "No? Tough!
You're the official photographer now, so here's the camera. Figure it out." Had I missed getting the picture? "Go back and get
another one." And a deadline was a deadline was a deadline.
David was my very own Lou Grant.

At midday, I was invited to join his family for lunch since
there was nowhere else nearby to eat. David's young daughter, Carolyn, would tell us about her classmates at school while
George, the adorable toddler, showed off his toys. Watching my
gruff editor as a loving father undercut the toughness he tried
to make me believe was his natural state of being. Money was
scarce, since the Bentleys had poured everything into their new
venture. Their efforts would eventually pay off big time for them
when the *B-S News* became the *Daily News* of Halifax and the
founders were handsomely bought out after a few years of giving
the local daily, the *Chronicle-Herald*, a run for its money.

• • •

I met another Lou Grant when I began journalism school. His
name was Joe Scanlon. Joe's reputation as a hard-ass journalism
professor crossed borders. Years later, when I became friendly

with a Thai journalist who had attended Carleton on a Rotary international scholarship, the first words out of her mouth about our alma mater were "Did you have that horrible Joe Scanlon as a prof?" We contemplated creating an "I hated Joe Scanlon" alumni club.

Joe wasn't so much horrible as an old-school front-page journo. To be fair, he did instill in his students, including me, some fundamental values that would be useful when we began working as reporters. Like David Bentley had, Joe insisted we return to the scene of any interview if we'd missed asking the right questions, even if that meant running across the Carleton campus in a blizzard. (Turns out there was a reason the university was connected by a maze of tunnels. Their purpose had baffled me when I first arrived.) But Joe could be a complete jerk too. Once, he made me write, rewrite, and rewrite again a radio story he had assigned to our class for no better reason than to see how long it would be before I told him to piss off. After I swore at him and ripped my copy paper into tiny pieces, Joe told me I had spunk, just as the television Lou Grant had famously said to Mary Richards. And just like Lou, he added, to much laughter from my classmates, "I hate spunk."

Besides persistence, that year I acquired another skill that would help me as a woman in journalism. I learned how to order a man's drink: scotch, neat, instead of a Dubonnet on the rocks with a twist of lemon. My conversion to the hard stuff happened during a national leadership convention for the Conservative Party of Canada being held in Ottawa. A bunch of us student journalists were recruited to run errands for the real ones covering the event for CTV, one of Canada's national television networks. We ended up drinking at the bar in the National Press Club. After the patronizing looks I received while ordering my usual libation, I choked down a scotch the second time around—and never ordered a girly drink again.

• • •

I spent half a dozen years as a reporter for the radio and television news service of Canada's public broadcaster, the CBC, beginning as an editorial assistant in Halifax. I was back on the east coast visiting friends when I heard there was a temporary opening in the CBC Television newsroom. I pounced with my resumé. When I demonstrated in that position that I had some news sense, thanks to both of my mentors, I was hired as a full-time reporter in Winnipeg. The token woman there had moved on and a replacement was needed. I quickly learned that the men got all the best assignments and all the overtime pay too. My news director told me outright that my married male colleagues with mortgages deserved the extra pay more than I did as a young single woman.

Since the serious, "hard news" assignments went to the male reporters, the "soft news" was assigned to me. That included the act-of-God stories, and in Winnipeg there were many of those: floods, snowstorms, mosquitoes, locusts. (I'm kidding about the locusts, although sometimes in plague season it felt like they could descend at any time.) I was stuck on the disaster beat until I pitched the idea to report regularly on the northern part of Manitoba. No one else was keen to develop that beat, and since I was stuck covering frog-jumping contests (true story), I kept a sharp eye out for opportunities.

Soon I was on the road most of the time, travelling with a cameraman to places such as The Pas and Churchill. Trying to capture footage of the famous polar bears in Churchill's forty-below temperatures was challenging. Once, while I was recording an on-camera closing to one of my dispatches, an artic wind froze my mouth and caused my glasses to fall off my face, snapped right in two. I twice visited Flin Flon, known for hockey players and fishing, to cover its annual trout festival, returning to Winnipeg both times with fresh fillets in my purse. A highlight was flying into Lynn Lake for a day to interview the *For Better or For Worse* cartoonist Lynn Johnston. She had settled in the northern Manitoba town to draw her popular cartoon strip.

I also began covering what were then referred to in mainstream media as "Native issues." That shift in focus meant not all of my northern trips were as straightforward as attending a fishing derby. Many of the stories I covered were downright disheartening. And they were an eye-opener for a sheltered Jewish girl from Toronto who had grown up unaware of the horrors Indigenous children endured after being ripped from their families and forced to attend the notorious residential schools. I was ignorant of intergenerational family trauma and alcohol abuse, just two of many destructive legacies of an inhumane system.

One particular story took me to Norway House, a community 460 kilometres north of Winnipeg. Named for the Norwegians hired to labour for the Hudson's Bay Company, Norway House had once been an important hub for the company's fur trade. It was well known for its fishing and hunting, as well as the production of boats. By the time I visited in the late seventies, Norway House was struggling with multiple economic and social challenges. Things had gotten so bad that a large delegation of townspeople staged a weeks-long protest at the provincial legislature in Winnipeg to get their concerns heard. My newsroom colleagues had covered those protests and not very sympathetically.

When I visited Norway House a few months later to follow up, intending to show our viewers what had prompted the protests, my cameraman and I were not exactly welcomed with open arms. Who could blame people? But that didn't excuse what happened to us. We were threatened by a group of locals angry at our network and had to get the hell out of town quickly, in the dead of night.

When we returned to Winnipeg, my news director (the same idiot who had made the comment about only men deserving overtime pay) called me into his office to discuss what had happened. Instead of reassuring me that the network would investigate the incident, he said, "Well, now you know why we don't want to send women reporters up north." I challenged him but didn't mention that I'd been threatened with personal assault. That would have been pointless. I had previously complained to him that someone in our newsroom was harassing me late at night with phone calls ending in hang-ups, scaring the hell out of me. I was living in a basement apartment without much security. He hadn't believed me then, and I doubted I would get any further in this instance. He didn't want to know. No one did.

As a parting shot, I decided to offer a piece of unsolicited advice. "And here's a thought," I said to him as I was leaving his office. "Why don't we train an actual Native journalist to cover their own issues, instead of sending up someone who looks like me?" I told him I would happily train my own replacement. Eventually, more Indigenous journalists would work in the newsroom, but in the meantime, I carried on reporting from the North.

· · ·

I may have been quick out of the gate at launching my reporting career, but I had missed an important generational milestone: I hadn't travelled internationally yet. At twenty-five, I didn't even have a passport. To close that gap in my experience, I requested and was granted a six-month leave of absence from the CBC in Winnipeg. Off I went, on my own. By that time, most of my potential travel companions had already returned from their own Grand Tours. I planned to study French in France after a few months of touring around Northern Europe. Unfortunately, my trip failed to unfold that way. By the time I got to Paris, I was formally declaring myself a failure as a traveller. A host of setbacks had culminated in the ultimate one: because of an infection on my foot, I could barely walk. I would have to go home.

But where was home? I flew to Toronto to stay with family, but my furniture and belongings were in Winnipeg, where my job was being filled by someone else during my leave. Still limping, I found a temporary reporting position in the CBC TV newsroom in Windsor, Ontario, across the river from Detroit. The automotive reporter there was about to begin an extended sick leave. I didn't know very much about the automotive industry, but I accepted the job anyway.

My first assignment was attending a news conference called by long-time Ford executive Lee Iacocca to announce his jump to

Chrysler. What could I possibly ask? And who the hell was Lee Iacocca, anyway? Before heading out to Detroit from Windsor with a cameraman, I discussed my concerns with my assignment editor.

"Oh, you don't actually have to know anything," he assured me. "Just ask how the announcement will affect the Canadian operation."

Sounded easy, so I did just that. I followed the same advice when I found myself in a scrum of Detroit reporters vying for the attention of Henry Ford II. I can't remember what Ford was up to, but I do recall shouting "How will this impact Ford Canada?" at the great man while a swarm of male reporters tried to elbow me out of the way. Henry Ford II was known for his tipple, and he had clearly been into the booze already on that day. He was so surprised when a young woman with curly hair popped up and stuck a microphone in front of him that he said something he wasn't supposed to say. By the time I got back to the Canadian side of the border, his PR handlers had already been in touch with my newsroom editors to "clarify" the sound bite Ford had given me.

When my Windsor gig was up, I headed back to my furniture and permanent job in Winnipeg. I spent another year working as a reporter in the CBC TV newsroom as the northern reporter before being made a host on the evening news show *24 Hours*. It was by far the best opportunity in my career to date. But life decided to intervene. I fell in love, and just as my father had predicted on that long-ago evening over Chinese food, I shifted to freelancing from wherever I happened to be in the world. This particular Mary Richards didn't just get married. She ended up leaving the country. Lou always said she had spunk.

Thou Shalt Not Marry Outside the Tribe

IS HE JEWISH? Forget about the Ten Commandments. In the world I grew up in, thou shalt marry Mr. Jewish Right was the unofficial eleventh. My tribe boxed me into a dating ghetto when I was a teenager and warned me none too subtly to stay there. Their efforts to see me properly married to a nice Jewish boy were supported by Jewish youth organizations, summers spent at Jewish camps, and, in the days before apps like JDate, the matchmaking services of my aunt Beryl. Well-meaning, of course, she led the charge among my aunties to fix me up every time I visited Toronto after leaving home. Those blind dates never ended well.

Helping to keep me penned in were the haunting conversations I'd overheard among adults from an early age. They might mention how the daughter of so-and-so had disgraced her family by marrying someone *who is not Jewish*—words more shuddered than spoken, with the level of disapproval others reserved for drug dealers or child molesters. The message could not have been more clear: for a woman who married outside our faith, there were consequences.

The stress of these dating limitations grew even more following the 1985 publication of a demographic study called

"Marriage Patterns in the United States." The study would eventually be exposed as one of the biggest fake news stories of the eighties, but its dubious findings had been floating around years earlier. Supposedly, a white, college-educated woman born in the mid-1950s who was still single by age thirty had only a 20 percent chance of marrying. By the age of thirty-five, her odds dropped to 5 percent. The punchline? A forty-year-old single woman was more likely to be killed by a terrorist than to find a husband. Narrow those odds to a subset of the species, a *Jewish* single woman seeking a Jewish husband, and even Vegas bookies would be loath to take bets on the outcome.

With the imperative of my birthright in mind, I knew that the gorgeous *goyishe* guy with the impossibly white-bread name of Rodney Briggs, sitting across a table from me one October 1980 evening in Winnipeg, was not the man I was supposed to marry. That we were on a date at all was a surprise. The first time we met, at a dinner party at the home of a mutual friend, Rodney hadn't exactly been smitten with me. In high spirits after gorging on paella and sangria, I had got down on the floor to perform for my fellow diners a ridiculous skit I had just seen on *The Gong Show*. Like the talent show contestant had done, I imitated a piece of bacon frying by lying flat on my back and twitching, as if the floor were a frying pan. Rodney was not impressed, and it would be three years before our paths crossed again at another dinner party. I happened to be there with a friend of his when Rodney arrived, looking miserable. He had just broken up for the zillionth time with his girlfriend. When he caught sight of me, his eyes lit up. So did mine. Soon his friend was toast and the frying bacon was forgotten altogether.

• • •

Rodney entertained me on our first date with tales of hitchhiking through Africa and learning to speak Spanish in Guatemala. I fell hard—not only for him but also for all the places I imagined he could take me. It didn't hurt that, to me at least, he looked like a young Robert Redford with a beard. When he shared his dream to join Canada's foreign service and live overseas, I said something inane like "That sounds divine!" (Flirting was never my strong suit.) That I was an inexperienced traveller was obvious from my own pathetic stories. But the jig was definitely up when I asked: "What exactly is the foreign service, anyway? Is it like the foreign legion?" My date laughed his head off. I was cute back then.

Six months later, Rodney asked me to marry him while we were picking up bagels on an ordinary Saturday morning. A delicatessen in Winnipeg may not have been the most romantic of venues, but it certainly had the element of surprise. What Gentile proposes while buying lox and cream cheese? I had not dared to think how serious the two of us had become until he popped the question. Sort of. As we navigated the aisles, searching for chopped herring, Rodney explained he had received official word the day before that he had been accepted into the foreign service. The job offer meant he would have to be in Ottawa by the summer. We should move there together, he said as a statement of fact, not a question. And, oh yes, it made perfect sense for us to become engaged. Another pronouncement.

None of the store's other patrons would have guessed what was transpiring between us. My companion had not fallen to his knees, presented a diamond engagement ring, or shown any public display of affection. We could have been discussing the weather, for all anyone knew, although in Winnipeg, where temperatures drop to forty below in the winter, conversations about the forecast *are* important. Even *I* almost missed the proposal. I was preoccupied with the thought that I'd have to leave my current post, the best journalism job I had ever had, to join him in Ottawa when I heard the word *engaged*.

Rodney's emotional affect is like the famous *New Yorker* cartoon of an Irish setter that wears the same facial expression in three different panels. Happy, sad, shocked—the dog is deadpan in all three. I found the lack of visual clues to Rodney's moods and feelings confusing. His expressionless nature comes from the stoic British heritage of his parents and could not be more different from the way I grew up—with family and friends telegraphing their emotions on their faces, with their body language, and with words that often felt like they were being shouted from a megaphone. Compared to that, his calm demeanour communicated nothing.

"Did you just ask me to marry you?"

"Yes, I guess I did."

Pause.

"Okay. Yes. I will marry you, Rodney Briggs. Oh, there are the kosher dills we've been looking for. Grab a jar, would you please?"

• • •

I called my father right away with the news. My expectations of any excitement from Toronto were low. Still, my voice couldn't conceal my happiness.

"I'm in love, Dad! And we're engaged!"

"Is he Jewish?"

"Well, no."

"I see. Just to be clear, then, I am not giving you a wedding."

His reaction was not solely because of the mixed marriage, although that gave him cover.

"I know, Dad. Unlike your poker buddies, you don't plan to go broke just to give your daughter away. You've been telling me that since I was a little girl."

"Maybe I will give you a small party," he said, softening his tone.

"Not necessary, Dad. Just be happy for me. Please."

I had never pictured myself in a bridal gown. Donning a veil and walking down the aisle in high heels with all eyes on me was the stuff of my nightmares, not my dreams. My father would have to come up with other ways to hurt me. Unfortunately, he found plenty of them. The first was placing a wedding announcement in a Toronto newspaper and then informing me that not a single person had called to wish him *mazel tov*. There was not much joy from Rodney's side either. Our engagement was a giant elephant that joined us for dinner with his parents in Winnipeg and was ignored while we all drank too much. My mother-in-law did bring me a little celebratory present: a container of liquid soap she'd bought at the drugstore on the way to the restaurant.

I had won the trifecta of bad luck with mother figures: a dead one at the age of twelve; an insecure stepmother after my father remarried when I was a teenager; and now, in my twenties, a cold and indifferent mother-in-law who asked her son if he was eating a lot of Jewish food after spotting a loaf of rye bread on his kitchen counter.

We were married by a family court judge in 1981, not long after the summer's fairy-tale wedding between Prince Charles and Lady Diana. Rodney and I had fewer guests—my brother Laurie and his wife Carol were the sole witnesses—amid a lot less pomp. I wore a short ivory-coloured silk dress I'd purchased months earlier for the wedding of an old friend of Rodney's, and I picked up some flowers to carry at a nearby mall. I clutched a lovely monogrammed handkerchief that had belonged to my late mother.

The Prince of Wales may have glided to his wedding in a 1902 State landau and his bride ridden there in a glass coach. We arrived at the courthouse in the beat-up Mazda I had bought when I first moved to Winnipeg. The plugs for warming the interior and the engine hung out the front of the car, and frost shields covered the windows. There was no one to wave at anyway.

The last time I saw my father alive, almost twenty years after my phone call to announce my engagement, he was still sheepish about his response. Over the years, his failure to help me celebrate my marriage among family and friends had become a running joke between us.

"Are you ever going to forgive me for not giving you a wedding, Rob?"

"Nope."

We laughed about it, as we always did. I could never hate him. And besides, as I often pointed out to him, I might not have had the big wedding, but I got the marriage. And we all know how that particular royal wedding turned out.

A Newsroom of One

RODNEY AND I left Ottawa for a subsidized honeymoon in New York City two weeks after we were joined in civil matrimony. He had been selected, along with a dozen other new foreign service recruits, to fetch coffee for his elders during the twelve-week fall session of the United Nations General Assembly. We were assigned a small, one-bedroom suite with a kitchenette on the tenth floor of the Plaza Fifty Hotel in Midtown Manhattan, within walking distance of the UN. From one window, we could see the backside of the iconic Waldorf Astoria hotel. From another, we looked out at a fire escape, often with some dodgy-looking people lurking on it. Both views were very NYC.

In the early eighties, the Big Apple was not exactly a safe city. Taking a graffiti-covered subway train or even walking in what seemed like genteel, well-lit places was not always wise, especially after hours. Times Square had not yet been cleaned up. After catching shows on Broadway, we would walk back to our hotel at high speed, making eye contact with no one. I had never seen so many people living on the street. It was disturbing to witness such despair alongside five-star restaurants, classy brownstones, and shiny black stretch limousines.

Yet the obvious poverty also made us feel rich. I no longer had a well-paid television job, but Rodney and I were able to do much on very little. The weekly expenses stipend of US$150 he received from the government every Friday in cash might have been a million dollars. We dined frugally during the week, living on slices from New York's famous Ray's Pizza or sharing brisket sandwiches from the corner deli. But when Friday arrived, we were lining up for half-price tickets for Broadway shows or riding the Staten Island Ferry for next to nothing. And we were in love. Life couldn't get much better. I just had to figure out the work thing.

When I decided to marry Rodney, the *Winnipeg Free Press* thought my engagement newsworthy enough for a story, which it ran with the headline "Pascoe Gives Up 24 Hours to Follow Fiancé." I responded with an angry letter to the editor. I was hardly "giving up" anything except mosquitoes, forty-below temperatures in the winter, and floods in the spring, but I didn't put that in my letter. What I did say was that I was *gaining* a world of opportunities. Even with my father's infuriating prediction ringing in my head, choosing Rodney over my career had been a no-brainer. I focused on the bright side of giving up a great gig: the UN would be my first important leap from local to global.

I arrived in New York City naively thinking I would be able to freelance, something new for me. But I hadn't counted on having a crisis of confidence—and not just over my abilities as a reporter. Before I could even get to pitching stories to news organizations, I needed a professional persona. It felt so much easier to watch humanity from high above, on the tenth floor, than to join the streaming mass of people at street level, all of whom looked so bloody self-assured. The endless parade of well-dressed career women intimidated me. Many wore sneakers with their corporate suits, a fashion fad at the time, while carrying their heels in giant tote bags, and they all sported the seriously shellacked giant hairdos of the day. Their shoulder pads could have stopped an opposing football team, and their take-no-prisoners demeanour included a daunting ability to make eye contact with even lowly hicks like me. I wanted what those fabulously confident women were wearing and carrying, and I would take their sense of self too, while I was at it.

·   ·   ·

A few days into our New York honeymoon, Rodney put on the three-piece suit he'd been married in, a bespoke diplomat's pinstripe that was a gift from his father, and headed to the offices of the Permanent Mission of Canada to the United Nations. I fussed over what I should wear, settling finally on a skirt and a jacket armed with extra-large shoulder pads, and headed out to meet the CBC Radio producer I'd contacted. Her office was in the Secretariat Building, where the press corps was housed to be close to the General Assembly Hall. An elegant European woman in her early forties, the producer was a long-time United Nations hand who exuded experience.

The first question she asked me seemed simple. "How long will you be here?"

"Oh," I said, "we're here for three months, for the General Assembly."

"No," she said. "I meant, how long will you be here *today*?"

Unsure where this was leading, I thought fast. "I'm here as long as you want me to be."

"Good," she said. "This is what I would like you to do. I need you to listen to the speech on agriculture that a representative from the Soviet Bloc is going to give shortly (you can watch it on that monitor over there), then write a sixty-second voicer that we will record and file to *The World at Noon*. Do you think you can do that?"

Huh? I said to myself, wondering if I could possibly deliver what she'd asked.

"No problem," I said aloud. Thankfully, the ability to bluff was already part of my journalism tool kit.

Instead of offering me headphones, she turned up the volume on the monitor and handed me a pen. Then: "I'll leave you to it."

How hard can this be? I thought. And how lucky am I to have been given an assignment on my first day? This is going to be great. Yes, great. Wait, the guy has started speaking and I'm not sure that's English. Hey! Is there a simultaneous translation thingy I'm supposed to be wearing? Wait a minute, that *is* English he's speaking. Just very accented. Pay attention. Concentrate.

Wait, isn't that Rodney?

Sure enough, as the camera panned the General Assembly Hall, I could see my new husband sitting at the Canada table looking as dazed and confused as I felt. He had obviously been sent as a placeholder for the cameras.

"Hey, everyone. Anyone! That's my husband of two weeks over there!" I was speaking to an empty room until the producer came by to check up on me, carrying a sheet of paper.

"I forgot to give you this," she said. The paper turned out to be a press release about the speech. I noted, thankfully, that I could use it to fake my way through the voice report.

I started to tell her about seeing Rodney. It took me a few minutes to register that she wasn't smiling. "Your husband works for the Canadian mission?" I was sure I had told her this, but apparently she had not heard. "We will discuss that later. First we record the story." *Uh-oh.*

Afterwards, leaving the Secretariat Building to head back to our hotel, I spotted Rodney coming up an escalator as I was going down one. We each blurted out the same thing: "You can't believe the morning I've just had! Can't wait to tell you later!"

Could this really be happening? Could I really be making it already in New York City? Of course not. Despite movie sets around every corner, this particular heroine did not suddenly rise from obscure freelancer to UN correspondent. The next time I contacted the producer, hoping for another assignment, she told me that being married to someone in the Canadian diplomatic service disqualified me from reporting from the UN. Maybe, she suggested, I should head over to Park Avenue, where the CBC had another office, for soft feature stories of a non-political nature. And so I went from filing for *The World at Noon* to freelancing for *The Food Show* on CBC Radio. Not that there was anything wrong with that.

• • •

When Rodney and I moved to Bangkok for his first posting in the early eighties, my prospects in journalism encountered the same Catch-22 I had faced in New York. Working as a news correspondent, covering anything political, required press credentials. And as a diplomatic spouse, I was denied access to those credentials.

That was discouraging, because we had moved to Southeast Asia in very interesting times for a journalist. The Vietnam War and the killing fields of Cambodia, then called Kampuchea, had left thousands of refugees in camps along the border. Between 1975 and 1982, Canada would resettle more than 120,000 Vietnamese refugees in the largest humanitarian effort my country had ever undertaken. As part of Rodney's work at the Canadian embassy in Bangkok, he visited refugee camps every week to identify potential candidates for a family reunification program. I toured one camp with him but became pregnant with our daughter, Lilly, soon after. Even the refugee story remained beyond my reach.

Instead, after a brief flirtation with fiction that was more therapeutic than literary, I became a freelance feature writer, selling stories to regional publications. They weren't important investigative pieces about secret bombings in Laos. However, at least I was writing *something*, mostly book reviews and articles for airline magazines like Thai Airways' inflight *Sawasdee* magazine. One piece that became extremely popular, "A Woman in Bangkok," was a shopping guide for female visitors to a country that, let's face it, catered to men. After that, whenever friends-of-friends-of-friends visited Thailand and insisted I personally take them shopping, an activity I hated, I just handed them a copy of the article.

Pitching silly travel pieces ("Tuk-Tuk Tips" comes embarrassingly to mind) was not quite how I'd imagined my career unfolding. In the first year of our posting, I tried to convince the Bangkok bureau chief of *Time* magazine to hire me for the stringer's job he was trying to fill. I arrived at his home seven months pregnant, dripping from head to toe from the short walk to his place, my sample news clippings drenched and unreadable in my hand. He handed me a glass of water. I wanted to throw it on my face. I didn't get the job.

I craved an opportunity to combine my chosen profession with a purpose. One arrived a few months after our daughter was born, during a regular follow-up visit to my Thai obstetrician.

"Do you have a few extra minutes for a chat?" Dr. Tanit asked when we were through. Lingering in his office after my checkup was a pleasure. All of the foreign moms he delivered fell a little bit in love with him, me included. His manner was so gentle and his smile so genuine, he was hard to resist.

"I understand you are a journalist," he began.

"Yes, I am," I replied, feeling chuffed that he knew. "But I don't feel much like one anymore."

"I may have something that will interest you." He explained that his wife, Mel, a British midwife who had taught me pre-natal exercises, had founded a support group for international mothers. "Mel could really use a journalist to help her create a newsletter," he said. Was I interested? Hell, yes.

In those days before the internet, a newsletter full of advice and humour about motherhood abroad was a lifesaver. And not only for the other mothers. Writing it saved *me*. Volunteering alongside my best friend Mary, another new mom and fellow Canadian, I wrote words that were useful and that resonated emotionally. By the time I left Bangkok, I had turned that newsletter into a monthly magazine. It's still being published decades later.

The universe had rewarded me and not just with the newsletter. I now had an idea and a road map to my holy grail: a book.

A Broad Abroad

RODNEY HAD BEEN studying Mandarin in Ottawa for a full year before the political confrontation that ended so badly in Beijing's Tiananmen Square in June 1989. Numerous countries recalled their diplomats, joint business ventures were put on hold, and bilateral relationships were reassessed. Overnight, China was not the same country Rodney had been preparing for. A second year of language study lay ahead, but instead of sending us to Hong Kong for that, as had been the custom in the past, Rodney's bosses decided to make him a test case by sending him to the "other" China, Taiwan. Would a Canadian working out of the small trade office there cause any kind of reaction? (Spoiler alert: no one even noticed.)

Canada has no formal diplomatic relations with Taiwan, so we would receive only a bare minimum of support from the government. The trial posting would certainly have been easier if we had been going just as a couple. But by then we had two young children in tow. On top of that, Rodney gave me the news of this bait and switch from Hong Kong to Taipei only four months before we were set to leave Canada. I had to hustle to schedule the surgery my doctor had recommended I have before we left, a partial hysterectomy—no picnic at the best of times.

Just to recap: We were not going where I'd thought we would be going and I had absolutely no say in the matter. Political events were convulsing around us and blaring from television sets, scaring our friends and relations. I was headed for major surgery that would end my child-bearing years at thirty-six and faced at least a six-week recovery, after which I would have to pack up our household and move our family of four to the other side of the world. No time to get emotional about anything, as was the way of our marriage. Yet how motivating it can be to feel screwed over by circumstances beyond your control.

Within days of moving into our Taipei apartment, I was writing in earnest about the experience of moving overseas with a husband. I wanted other wives to know what they were *really* getting into. No one had ever written an honest, blunt book devoted entirely to the wife's perspective before. I called my manuscript *A Broad Abroad*. After reading some early chapters, Rodney began referring to it as my *manifesto*. By the time we moved to Beijing in the fall of 1990, I had a solid first draft in hand.

• • •

Beijing was an improvement over Taipei as far as postings went, because we had the welcome support of the Canadian embassy. However, the apartment we'd been assigned in a diplomatic compound wasn't nearly as nice as what we had left behind. It was dark, dusty, and depressing. Fortunately, everyone lived in similar surroundings, which contributed to a very strong esprit de corps.

It was a given that we were being listened to on the black rotary phone in the hallway. Still, the phone linked us to the outside world. And it was on that ancient device that I learned I was about to become a published author.

The four of us had been enjoying an ordinary, middle-of-the-week banquet prepared by Mr. Wong, our cook, who is probably running a successful restaurant today somewhere in a more upscale Beijing. When we heard the phone ring, Mr. Wong went to answer it.

"Madam. Phone for you. Singapore is calling."

"Singapore? Do I know anyone by that name?" I winked at my kids as I said it, but then I remembered. A few months earlier, on a visit to a bookstore in Hong Kong, I had spotted a series titled Culture Shock! I thought the publisher might be interested in my book, since it was all about the culture shock experienced by expat wives. I had sent the manuscript off to them in Singapore, and then, hearing nothing back, mailed copies to half a dozen American publishers. The premier cross-cultural press had already rejected me, telling me in essence: *Wives—who cares?* Now, someone named Singapore was on the line. What were the chances?

"Hello, Robin," said a female voice with just the hint of a British accent. "I'm the managing editor at Times Publishing. I apologize profusely for this, but your manuscript was at the bottom of a pile on my desk. I only discovered it today, while preparing to leave for BookExpo America in New York. We want to publish it."

It took me a minute to find my voice. "So you see the importance of addressing the culture shock of expat wives?" I said, feeling my heart begin to race. "How wonderful. I'm thinking of writing a companion book about the culture shock faced by parents who move with their children overseas."

"We want to publish that one too," she replied without a moment's hesitation. "Can you give me a fax number so I can send you a contract right away? And how soon can you send me the latest, most complete version of your wife book?"

"In a few days," I promised.

I had my work cut out for me. I hadn't looked at the manuscript in months. But *my book was going to be published!* I started to shake and cry, crumpling into a mess right there in the hall.

"Madam?" Mr. Wong was at my side immediately, the concern on his face making me cry even harder. He returned to the kitchen, only to emerge moments later. On a lacquered tray I had bought at the Friendship Store close to our compound, he was carrying a stiff drink of scotch and a fresh pack of cigarettes from the duty-free store. He carefully opened the pack, handed me a cigarette, and, with the widest grin on his face, offered me a light.

I celebrated my thirty-eighth birthday holed up, chain-smoking, completing my revisions in a windowless mah-jong room at our local health club. I used the same unconventional workspace to complete the second manuscript I had promised, about expat parents. The first book, which the publishers titled *The Wife's Guide to Successful Living Abroad*, was published in 1992, the year we finished our assignment to China.

• • •

Pushback to my book came swiftly from the corporate world. Company human resource types did not want wives encouraged by anyone to say, "I'm not going, dear." They wanted their male employees in those new jobs overseas yesterday, and the families (that is, the wives) were just supposed to get with the program.

A company's bottom line took a hit if an assignment went sideways because a family failed to thrive. That could be rectified with some simple, inexpensive support programs, my book argued. Language and cross-cultural training would be helpful, and for the spouse, some assistance to keep her career on track. It wasn't rocket science, but my ideas were deemed too radical.

I penned an op-ed piece intended for the *Asian Wall Street Journal*, my first attempt to communicate on the subject in the mainstream press. It was accepted, but a friend who worked for the newspaper told me later what had happened. A male editor in Hong Kong had tossed my piece into the garbage, but another editor, a woman, retrieved it, dusted it off, and published it. My article appeared in all of the paper's global editions, including in New York. It went on to be quoted in the academic international business management literature. My basic premise? Companies could save millions of dollars by spending a few thousand on life support for expat families. Radical indeed.

The resistance was even worse, and more hurtful, when my Singapore publisher sold North American rights to a US publisher. The American publisher demanded changes, beginning with the title, *The Wife's Guide to Successful Living Abroad*. If the original publisher had kept my funnier title, *A Broad Abroad*, it might have made things easier.

The feminist publishing police of the 1990s were woefully uninformed about expat life. According to them, an equal number of men and women played the role of accompanying partner. That may be what expat life looks like today, but the number of male non-working spouses at that time was infinitesimal (and those males were already getting special treatment). Besides,

I had written my book for women, and it was *supposed* to be both irreverent and informative. If your career couldn't go anywhere during an overseas posting and you were of child-bearing age, go ahead and have a baby, I advised. Nope. The US publisher wanted to change that and change the book's title to *A Spouse's Guide*. I refused.

A Wife's Guide ended up being labelled a problem book, and it was hard to find in bookstores. Luckily, many expat women were desperate to hear what I was saying, and somehow they managed to find it.

• • •

Amazon, the giant online bookstore that would eventually change everything, had not yet been launched when, in 1993, I attended a conference in London called Women on the Move. Attendees were primarily expat women moving around with their husbands. (No one was telling *them* to call themselves "spouses on the move." Just saying.) By that time, a British publisher had bought the rights to my two Culture Shock! titles (*A Parent's Guide* had since been finished and released) and had no problem with my point of view. Both books were selling well in Britain, and there were tons of copies for sale at the conference. The opening keynote speaker referenced my first book multiple times, which was both gratifying and vindicating. The conference bookstore sold out of both titles.

I took the opportunity while in London to network with various organizations that prepared families for overseas assignments. At the end of a long day, I pitched up, as the Brits say, at the London bureau of CNN for an interview about the controversy surrounding my first book. I had called in a favour from an old CBC Windsor friend who knew the CNN evening anchor in London. I was accompanied by my friend Liz, another foreign service wife, with whom I was staying.

This being the UK, we had been on several trains that day, and I looked the worse for wear. My hair was windblown and my makeup—applied before dawn, when we had first set out—had all but disappeared. Liz reassured me that a makeup artist would soon fix me up. Since we were delayed in arriving, though, I ended up going straight into the studio. I only had time enough to grouse when the production assistant removed the necklace I was wearing, some colourful beads, because it would interfere with the microphone she was clipping on me.

"That necklace was my only accessory," I whined to Liz, who, like me, was trying not to be awestruck by where we were standing.

"You always have your hair, Robin," she said and laughed. I didn't.

The anchor and I taped the interview, and I managed to get the point across that my book had put me in the crosshairs of both the corporate world and the publishing world. I had hoped to mention that some expat wives were not terribly pleased with what I had written either, claiming they had no idea what I was talking about. *They* had never experienced culture shock, and they couldn't be happier in their various husbands' postings. I had heard this enough times that I had crafted a comeback: "Wonderful. I hope you're helping others adjust, then. And oh, by the way, is that the third or fourth gin and tonic you're on now?" Unfortunately, there wasn't time to fit in my witty rejoinder.

My first book would eventually be published with its original title, *A Broad Abroad*, in 2009 by Expatriate Press, an imprint I created for my books. The resistance it faced had become less important to me after Rodney left the foreign service in 1996. His career had not progressed the way he had hoped, and when another opportunity presented itself, he accepted. We often wondered whether my book had had any impact on his career advancement, since he had heard through the grapevine that some senior Foreign Affairs types felt he had demonstrated a lack of judgment in "allowing" me to publish it. When he was informed that that was the prevailing view among his superiors, his response endeared him to me forever.

"Have you met my wife?"

Toasting a Haggis

NOT LONG AFTER we were posted to Seoul in 1994, I received a phone call from the local chieftain of the St. Andrew's Society. My first question to him, of course, was "What the heck is a chieftain?" It didn't sound very Korean. From his accent, he sounded Scottish, and St. Andrew's was another clue.

The caller's day job was running the Reuters news bureau in the South Korean capital, he explained. In his spare time, he served as the de facto president of the local chapter of the international organization devoted to all things Scottish. In that role, he was inviting me to deliver one of the toasts at the upcoming St. Andrew's Society ball. The annual event is a rowdy all-night celebration of Scottish heritage involving men in kilts, Scottish dancing, bagpipes, and a ceremonial sheep stomach called a haggis. While some people knew me as the author of two Culture Shock! titles, I was also the "Irreverent Expat" in one of the local English-language newspapers, the *Korea Times*. This was the title of a weekly humour column I had pitched for fun to the editor soon after we arrived. In that column, I mocked myself as much as other expats, and obviously, the chieftain figured I could offer something amusing for a toast.

Upon hearing the word *ball*, though, I almost bailed on the conversation. Seoul was supposed to be a *no ball post*. I had made this clear to my husband before we left Ottawa. After one too many depressing experiences with formal dress events, I had vowed never to attend another. I was simply too self-conscious about getting dressed up. Most of my expat girlfriends, wherever we happened to be living in the world, loved getting dresses made by seamstresses for special occasions. They spent hours in local markets searching for unique fabrics. I would rather have a root canal than browse mindlessly for buttons, and I consistently chose the wrong material. In the end, they would always look divine while I resembled a reupholstered sofa. What did I know? There had been no woman in the house during my formative years to teach me about clothes and I had flunked home economics. Once I almost lost a finger to an aggressive sewing machine.

Where there were Scots, though, there was sure to be good scotch, preferably old single malts, which happened to be my preferred drink. In spite of myself, I was intrigued by the invitation. "We've never had a woman deliver the toast on behalf of the guests before," the chieftain continued. "It would be fun to have you, if you would agree to come."

"Isn't there a lot of complicated Scottish dancing involved?" I asked. It was an important question. Rodney and I are utter failures in the dancing department. This distinction had been confirmed when we flunked a ballroom dancing course. One of us (and that would *not* be me) has absolutely no sense of rhythm.

"Aye, there's Scottish dancing," the chieftain said, "but you're not expected to participate." He hesitated for a moment. "Well, you will be asked to do the first dance. Don't worry, it's very easy. It's only the Gay Gordons." Like I knew what that was.

"With my husband as my partner? We're not very good dancers," I told him. I didn't even want to picture us attempting the dance. But the chieftain reassured me that I would not be opening the dancing with Rodney. I would dance with someone who had a lot more rhythm. And who'd be wearing a kilt.

• • •

For the next several weeks, I awakened every morning in a cold sweat. What had I gotten myself into? And what the heck was I going to wear? I had brought nothing with me from Canada that was suitable for such an event. And Seoul, in those years, did not have women's dress stores, fancy or casual, for foreigners like me. We shopped in the seconds and thirds knock-off markets of the Itaewon district. Not only would I have to write ten minutes of irreverent and hopefully funny remarks, but I would likely have to deliver them while wearing something god-awful.

Screwing up my courage, I visited Itaewon, dazed and stressed, wanting to buy something, *anything*, as quickly as possible. When I spotted a long, black crushed-velvet gown on a mannequin, I asked for it to be removed to see if it would fit me. It was tacky but a very simple design.

There were no changing rooms in the market, but vendors had fashioned a curtained space smaller than a telephone booth for that purpose. When I ventured out of my cone of privacy to find a mirror, the reflection confirmed that the look was as bad as I'd feared. But I was desperate, so I stopped to think. If I cut off the bottom half of the dress, threw it over black leggings, added the tall black suede boots I had owned for fifteen years (and which looked it) and as much costume jewellery as I could get my hands on, well, maybe the outfit would work. If not, I could always count on my wild curly hair to distract people from my appearance from the neck down.

I realized the moment we arrived at the ball that my look was too unconventional. Rodney and I mingled with men in tuxedos (*easy for them*) and women in elegant gowns, some with an added dash of tartan. As we entered the hotel ballroom, we spotted a couple we knew from the British embassy. After we exchanged greetings, they asked if we were Scottish dance aficionados.

"Actually, we're here so Robin can deliver one of the toasts," Rodney explained.

"Really? Well, that's very interesting," said the husband suspiciously.

"Very unusual," said his wife, not even trying to hide her surprise as she looked me up and down.

"Excuse me," I said to all three of them. I headed for the nearest ladies' room, where I promptly threw up.

• • •

I had promised Rodney I would not have a drop of booze until after I delivered my toast. I suppose he was looking out for my best interests, but I didn't appreciate that he kept an eye on me throughout the lengthy dinner and the rituals that followed, to make sure I stayed sober. Hours went by, until I just couldn't stand the pressure. With all eyes on the chieftain as he was making *his* toast, I managed to pour several fingers of the amazing single malt Aberlour into my water glass and set it down on the floor beside my chair. When I was called upon to deliver my toast, I grabbed the glass and, without making eye contact with Rodney, headed to the podium.

"Your chieftain promised me you would all be drunk as skunks by the time I got up here," I told my audience as an icebreaker. "Watching everyone from the top table over there, I think I can safely say he delivered on that promise!"

My remark prompted a round of applause.

"My husband," I said, pointing to Rodney, "suggested I try to get up here somewhat sober." A few snickers. "But to hell with that, I say." I raised my glass and, with an irreverent *l'chaim*, downed the fiery liquid. There was silent shock as I choked out the words: "Fair is fair."

I'd been asked to be politically incorrect, and there was no chance of my toast appearing on YouTube, since the World Wide Web was in its infancy. I opened with some choice insensitive remarks and slowly the applause began. At one point, I asked for another *wee dram* of the firewater and invited the audience to join me. That went over well, as did my comparison of the men in kilts to Canadian curlers: men with brooms. My big finish was sharing that I loved the sound of a Scottish accent in a man and found it sexy. I was mobbed after my toast by men anxious to flex their tongues.

I left the ball at 3:30 with Rodney at my side and a fresh bottle of Aberlour tucked under my arm. The minute we got home, my formal wear went into the trash. Fine single malts or not, there would be no more balls for me.

The Big Job

I'D NEVER HEARD the expression "a big job" before my girl-friend Jane introduced me to it one day. Jane is a fellow Canadian, a Maritimer from New Brunswick. She's ten years older than I am, which makes her a decade wiser. We became friends in South Korea in the mid-1990s, when we were both living there because of our husbands' careers.

On most weekday mornings, Jane and I walked and talked, side by side, on treadmills at the Seoul Club. Korean and expat members socialized and exercised there together, in keeping with the club's founding tradition. It had been created by royal charter in 1904 as a "convivial venue for international fellowship" by the Korean emperor, who donated a two-storey library on the grounds of one of his palaces for the purpose. By the time Jane and I were living in Seoul, the club had settled into a location fifteen minutes by car from Hannam-dong. That was the city district where Rodney and I lived with our two young children in our Canadian embassy–assigned staff quarters, a four-bedroom house long since bulldozed and replaced by high-rise apartments. Given the dense traffic in Seoul (something that never changes), the club felt as if it were practically around the corner, and even I could safely manage the simple drive there in our Hyundai Elantra.

Seoul is organized into a municipal grid of neighbourhoods and districts, each of them with street addresses that seem completely illogical (at least to outsiders). A house number did not follow naturally from the one beside it, and the signs for street names changed without warning. Yet the vague landmarks you needed for navigation could disappear overnight if a business went bankrupt or new construction moved in. We lived off Baskin Robbins Street, for example—not exactly an address that guaranteed a letter carrier would find us. The residence of the Mexican ambassador to South Korea happened to be right next door. That came in handy, and not just as another reference when giving out directions. For cocktail receptions, the Mexicans would often engage *mariachi* bands that entertained our sheltie, Sandy. He would bark at them for hours from the safety of our second-floor landing that overlooked their garden.

The Seoul Club sat directly across the street from Namsan Park, a delightful green space you are almost shocked to discover in the heart of that congested, polluted city of almost 10 million. Jane and I stubbornly stuck to our treadmills, though, instead of enjoying the cool fresh air offered by the shade of Namsan Mountain or inhaling the fragrant scent of the cherry blossom trees that bloomed in the park every spring. Looking back, I think we chose to remain indoors primarily to piss off a fellow club member, a retired Korean gentleman who had the luxury of exercising during the day. From his rowing machine close to our treadmills, he could be counted upon to give us the stink eye for our incessant chatter. We were happy to irritate the hell out of him.

One day, as our Korean eavesdropper shot us dirty looks, Jane and I discussed the career of a mutual friend back in Canada.

The friend in question was the important vice-president of some organization, the name of which escapes me now.

"She's one of those girls with a *big job*," Jane said, placing a heavy emphasis on the last two words. She didn't exactly spit them out, but she came pretty close. Being unfamiliar with the term, and guessing it had nothing to do with robbing a bank or performing a bodily function, I asked her for a definition.

"A *big job* is a very important one," she said. "At least, it *must* be terribly important, because there are so many meetings. It demands constant travel and endless late hours at the office. Women with big jobs are always exhausted. And they constantly remind the rest of us how tired they are because of their work." Jane took a moment to snort at the notion that a woman who only went to an office every day could possibly be more tired than one responsible for looking after a house full of children. Then she got to the heart of the matter, in her view, anyway.

"Women with *big jobs* always look very pulled together," Jane pronounced. "They wear high heels and power suits and carry designer briefcases." Jane has always been an elegant, well-dressed woman, even in her gym clothes. That made me suspect she disdained the sartorial more than the professional side of our mutual friend's exalted position in the working world.

We waved farewell to our annoyed observer and headed to the change room, the club's westernized version of a Korean public bathhouse, a *jjimjilbang*. As always, we enjoyed dipping into the by turns soothing and invigorating hot and cold tubs, and we were grateful we were two naked girlfriends (still talking, by the way), and not complete strangers scrubbing each other's backs.

As we showered and applied our makeup before heading home, we acknowledged that neither one of us really wanted to have a *big job*. But we agreed that Jane's wardrobe and sense of style put her chances of landing one way ahead of mine.

• • •

My reasons for rejecting the idea of a full-time, very important position were slightly more complicated than wardrobe challenges. Come hell or high water, I was determined to be waiting at home to greet Lilly and her younger brother Jay when they stepped off their school bus in the afternoon. Not for me being the mother who was still at her office, or out of the country all the time, or stuck in traffic on her way home during rush hour, too exhausted to chat with her kids when she finally arrived.

I wanted to be the kind of mother who sat down over a homemade snack and caught up on the news of her children's day while it was still fresh in their minds. If I had a *big job*, there was no way there could be freshly baked chocolate-chip yogurt banana Bundt cakes ready for after-school time. (Of course, I might also have been thinner.) My line was that I did this because they were children of the foreign service, constantly being uprooted during the first decade of their lives. If they were ever to feel settled, they needed some predictable routines. But really, it was about me as much as about my children. I wanted to be a mother they could rely on for my own reasons.

Some people found my ideas quaintly old-fashioned. They seemed especially retrograde to outsiders, given the feminist ambition and outrage that had consumed me during my youth. But when your values come from a painful place, like mine did, they are almost involuntary. They come from the heart, and mine was shattered early.

Even before she died, my mother had rarely been around to greet me at the end of the school day. I would come home on my own, making the fifteen-minute commute on foot from my elementary school—the kind of walk children were once allowed to do unescorted. If he didn't have band practice, my brother Laurie would arrive home soon after I did. He went to the high school I would eventually attend, about a half-hour walk from our house. Our mother would turn up later, sometimes with groceries in hand, perhaps still wearing her golf clothes. I have no memories of chatting with her about how my day had gone, but that might have been because I was too caught up in watching *The Commander Tom Show* on the local Buffalo TV station, WKBW, between *Adventures of Superman*. Laurie and I both loved the black-and-white serial. Our eldest brother, Michael, seven years my senior, remembers things differently. He says our mother was always at home after school. His memory conforms to his place in the birth order, though, as he was the privileged first born. Most of the pictures in our family photo albums seemed to be only of him.

Our mother, Bessie, was a 1950s middle-class housewife, the kind personified by the television moms on *Leave It to Beaver* and *The Donna Reed Show* (my own particular favourite, which my mother and I would watch together). I don't recall her wearing either pearls or an apron, though, and certainly not both at once, as those TV moms did. Most of Bessie's friends were just like her. They had stopped working outside the home when they married, often at their husbands' insistence, and they led busy lives managing their families, their households, and their social activities. My mother golfed on most days in the spring and summer, volunteered during the winter for Hadassah, the Jewish women's service organization, and in between played bridge and mah-jong. She spent hours reading pocketbooks, library books, and the books that arrived in the mail from the Book of the Month club.

Our house was cleaned by an endless rotation of Italian women, who all seemed to be widows named Maria dressed only in black. At exactly 5:20 every afternoon, Bessie would call my father's dental office to ask his nurse if Dr. Pascoe had left for home. Dinner was on the table like clockwork shortly after 6:00 p.m. When my father walked through our front door, she greeted him with a welcome home kiss. I doubt it even occurred to my mother to miss the nursing career of her premarital days.

Of course, there was more to her life than I could observe through a child's eye. For instance, my mother's parents came from Cape Breton to live with us for a while in Toronto when I was ten. My grandfather was undergoing treatment for lung cancer, and he slept in my bedroom while I bunked in with my grandmother in Laurie's bedroom. Laurie moved down to our basement to share a room, yet again, with Michael, but we all managed. I don't remember my mother displaying any tension during this visit, though she surely must have been feeling anxious. My grandfather died within six months. Barely two years later, Bessie herself would die prematurely. Considering how things turned out, it wasn't really so bad that I'd been left to fix my own snack after school or get started on my homework or practising the piano.

Rainy days had always been the exception when she was alive. On wet afternoons, I would leave school quickly, confident my mother would be waiting to drive me home. She never once disappointed me. In the lineup of cars, it was easy to spot her silver Vauxhall or her bright blue 1965 Comet. A rained-out golf game was probably the reason she was there, but that didn't matter. I knew I could count on her.

Once she was gone, I unravelled at the sight of the other moms' cars idling in the rain as they waited for my classmates. I would take off for home at high speed, crying as tears mixed with raindrops, ignoring anyone trying to catch up to me. I had a propensity for being overdramatic as a child, but on this matter I could be forgiven my histrionics. Will I ever forget my joy at jumping out of the rain and into my mother's car? At watching her stub out her ubiquitous cigarette in the ashtray, the tip circled with a ring of the red lipstick mothers wore in those days even to fetch children from school? And what about the sight of that unflattering, downright embarrassing accordion-style plastic bag on her head, the emergency rain bonnet she carried in her purse? It was always tied so neatly beneath her chin, as if a plastic bow would make it as fashionable as it was functional. The windshield wipers, swishing back and forth in the rain as her car idled, had a distinctive muffled sound that stays with me to this day.

Bessie was not a terribly affectionate woman. I have almost no memories of her hugs or kisses. But I do remember the intimacy we shared in the car.

Two lives were lost when she died: hers, and my own innocent life as a child. I suddenly became conscious of the existence of a "before time." Mine was set in a sporty 1960s car, on a rainy after-noon, with my mom in headgear she hoped would preserve her hairdo, lighting up yet another cigarette and shifting the car into gear to take me home. It was the safest place I would ever know.

I wanted my children to have a place like that in their memories of me one day. I was counting on a piece of banana cake, baked with love, to help me get my biggest job done.

• TWO •

Desperately Seeking Enlightenment

IN 1996, RODNEY left the diplomatic corps after fifteen years of foreign service for the Canadian government. Lilly would be heading for high school, and Jay had never really adjusted to moving around. It was the perfect time to exit the peripatetic life and put down roots in our own country. It also seemed an ideal moment for me to consult with a change guru. And I just happened to know of one.

Swami Shyam taught meditation and other self-awareness arts in a lost Shangri-La in the Himalayas. My cousin Daniel from Cape Breton, along with several hundred other Canadians, had been holed up with the swami since the mid-1970s at his ashram in Kullu, in the Indian state of Himachal Pradesh.

Rodney had been recruited from Seoul for a job in Vancouver, BC. His experience promoting Canada as an education destination to Korean foreign students had attracted the attention of the head of the Asia Pacific Foundation of Canada (APFC). The organization was taking over the foreign-student file from the federal government and Rodney was the perfect point person for the transition. Within a year, he would go on to create the not-for-profit Canadian Education Centre Network under the banner of the APFC and became its president.

Living on Canada's west coast would be a brand new experience. Neither of us had close family there, and we knew the city of Vancouver mainly as a quick stopover destination when travelling to and from Asia. We would also be adjusting to a different lifestyle. Given the glorious coastal mountains and ocean setting, Vancouver is all about the great outdoors, including skiing and year-round golf, and fitness is a quasi religion. Those expensive activities would present financial challenges, so our first order of business was to find an affordable place to live. Foreign Affairs made tickets available to us for that purpose, so Rodney suggested we take a house-hunting trip together. I could not imagine a more tedious exercise than looking at real estate. Any house can eventually be renovated, in my opinion, even if it takes several decades. I had another idea. "Can I use my ticket to go to India? I'd love to visit cousin Daniel at his ashram."

"If that's what you really want to do," replied Rodney. It's hard not to love a man who never says no to any of my travel ideas, no matter how crazy. Another husband might worry about his wife's safety, but not mine. He also knew I would be in good hands in India. Old foreign service friends of ours were attached to the Canadian High Commission in Delhi, and we could rely on them to get me out of any conceivable jam.

I concocted an "ashram wardrobe" at the clothing stalls of Itaewon. Daniel had sent instructions to dress modestly, so I selected long-sleeved tops and even longer flowing skirts. Completing my ensemble were a jean jacket, hiking boots, and a fanny pack—hippie throwback chic. I looked utterly ridiculous. I also bought a notebook to use as a travel diary, a box of good pens, and a generous supply of Imodium to fight the anticipated tummy bugs. I was ready for my India adventure. As for the house-hunting exercise, I had only one request. Whatever house my husband found, it had to be within walking distance of a quart of milk.

My friends were unanimous in their opinion that I had lost my mind. Curiously, they were not reacting to the idea of me seeking out a guru in India. Rather, they considered me insane to even think about moving into a house in such a pricey city without laying eyes on it first. Worse, I was trusting this decision to my husband. As for me, I never doubted that Rodney would find us a great place to live. Many years and multiple renovations later, we reside in the same wonderful home in North Vancouver— a ten-minute walk to a scenic mountain village with an excellent grocery store.

· · ·

Any seasoned traveller to the Indian subcontinent knows that overseas flights land in the middle of the night. That presents the first set of challenges a visitor must confront: deplaning half asleep and jet-lagged to crawl at a snail's pace through passport control and possibly search for missing luggage. When you finally exit the arrivals hall, you're bombarded with the chaos of shouting taxi drivers holding up signs, oppressive heat, combustible odours, and some very strange-looking conveyances to get you to your hotel.

I was not a seasoned solo traveller yet, so I was happy to spot a sign with my name on it. I had promised myself not to smoke on this trip but had already reneged on that during a stopover in Bangkok. Now I needed time to light up a cigarette before getting into the taxi waiting for me, arranged by Daniel's travel agent. It was a white Ambassador, the ubiquitous workhouse vehicle of India back then. I was excited to be staying, even overnight, at the famous Hotel Imperial, a monumental structure dating from the 1930s. Its grand renovation was a few years off, so a room there was still affordable. As its name implies, the hotel is a relic of the British Raj, with colonial ghosts still haunting its corridors.

The plan had been for the travel agent to meet me in the morning. Just as I was being dropped at the hotel's entrance, however, I learned from the taxi driver that the travel agent had changed careers, apparently while I was on my way from Seoul. The driver handed me my ticket for the flight from Delhi to the ashram and assured me I would have no problems finding my way to the domestic airport by taxi. The first thing I did after getting my room key was to find my way to the bar. Luckily, it was open all night.

· · ·

No booze would be allowed at the ashram, so I wasn't carrying even a drop of firewater to help curb my anxiety on the Archana Airways turboprop flight from Delhi to Kullu. That was probably a good thing, since there was no toilet on board either. Judging from my diary entry, written on the flight, I was already bursting with excitement.

Even from the tiny airplane window, the view was spectacular as we began our descent. Sitting at an altitude of 1,200 metres (almost 4,000 feet), Kullu has bragging rights to one of the most sublime settings in the Himalayas. It more than lives up to its moniker, the Valley of the Gods. As my guidebook informed me, tourists flocked to this hill station on the Kullu-Manali highway to enjoy its cool mountain air, hiking trails, and temples, and to take rafting trips on the River Beas, a holy river flowing through the states of Himachal Pradesh and the Punjab. I would discover soon that the river ran alongside the Vaishali Hotel, my home for the week to come. The sound of its rushing water would knock me out cold every night, a natural sedative I welcomed.

Daniel led the official delegation of about half a dozen people on hand to greet me at the small Kullu airport. It was many years since I had last seen him, and he looked well: in his mid-forties, he was trim and tanned, with the wide, beaming smile I remembered. He made me, a younger cousin by three years who had attended his bar mitzvah in Cape Breton as a little girl, feel like a visiting rock star, not a middle-aged woman in perimenopause. The women with him wore stunning Indian cottons draped with cashmere shawls and designer sunglasses.

The swami had attracted devoted Canadian admirers through a spiritual radio show he hosted in Montreal. Daniel and his friends had followed him when he returned to India. From very humble beginnings (they had slept under a tree for the first few years), the ashram now had several hundred followers who lived in an assortment of spaces, some just big enough for a bed and an altar for meditation. I was surprised to find the ashram located off a main street of Kullu and not, as I had anticipated, on an isolated mountaintop. There was even a Montreal dentist practising in their community, which no one seemed to find odd.

Daniel was the ashram's de facto general manager and the swami's right-hand man, which probably explained my royal welcome. I thought of his father, my uncle Mennie, who would have preferred that his youngest son use his management skills in the family grocery business back in Cape Breton. Happily, I would later be able to reassure my uncle that Daniel's talents were being put to good use.

• • •

Directly from the airport, with barely a moment to catch my breath, I was ushered into a room to sit on the floor alongside Swami Shyam's followers. A video camera held a prominent place in the room. Tea and some Indian snacks, unrecognizable to me, were served while we waited.

"You'll be granted an interview with Swamiji shortly," Daniel told me.

"All right," I said, getting right into the spirit of things. "About what?"

"Doesn't matter. He knows what you want to speak about with him."

"How does he know? Did you tell him anything?"

"No. Swamiji just knows. He's a knower."

Okey-dokey.

Swami Shyam entered and seated himself on a cushion facing his followers, looking as if he had just stepped out of central casting. An aging but spry sage with a long white beard, he was dressed in a flowing robe of bright turquoise. He giggled like the Dalai Lama, who lived a six-hour drive away in Dharamshala.

"So, Swamiji," I began, after I got the cue that we were rolling. "I'm in the middle of a life transition and struggling with my emotions, especially fear about the idea of my life going in a new direction. Your thoughts?"

"To understand change, you must understand unchange," he said. His smile was disarming. Was he smiling at me? At my question? At the beautiful day? At his followers? Their smiles were on such high beam they were burning a hole right through me. A bird chirped outside the window behind him, momentarily distracting me. *Pay attention, Robin!* The swami was going on and on about something which, for the life of me, I could not follow. I needed to be ready for whenever he stopped speaking, to ask another question. Except he never came to a full stop. Or even seemed to take a breath, for that matter. No one moved for what felt like hours. I had to pee so badly I thought I was going to burst. I couldn't help but wonder if everyone was wearing adult diapers to allow them to sit so long. *Focus, Robin!*

"Does that help?" the swami asked finally. My interview had ended. When Daniel sent me a transcript of Swami Shyam's disquisition later, I was amazed to discover that despite his flowery, often undecipherable language, his theories about unchange actually made sense. Well, sort of.

"Your teaching, Swamiji, is it that change has to come from within?" the transcript reports that I asked. (Apparently, I *had* managed to insert myself into the conversation.) "It is the unchange that intrigues me, if it is the unchange that will help people cope with change." I had been in Kullu barely a few hours and was already speaking in riddles.

•   •   •

My time at the ashram flew by in a blur of headache-inducing, elliptical conversations over hot beverages, taped interviews with the swami, and much sharing of family stories with Daniel as well as invigorating hikes. The video camera recorded the swami's every word for posterity. A visiting film producer from Bombay broke down dramatically during one of our daily group meetings, known as *satsang*, in a scene straight out of one of her Bollywood movies. Meanwhile, the swami's followers sat very still on their cushions, backs ramrod straight, sunglasses in place, in rapture over the torrent of words from their guru.

The bewildering words released into the fresh mountain air swaddled me like the cashmere shawl my cousin had given me to wear on my first evening. The sound lifted my spirits, much as I imagined a church choir must do when the faithful raise their voices together. *It has to be the elevation*, I told myself. There was no way I could be a believer after just a few days. But it was hard to resist this joyful utopia. And there was all that smiling.

It didn't matter that I avoided speaking about myself during *satsang*. On the second evening, my cousin insisted I share my observations—no matter how personal they were—by reading aloud from my diary, and I continued to do so every night to a different group. His request had been so guileless, it was easier to just acquiesce. I was basically singing for my meatless supper.

Amazingly, that diary would go on to have a life of its own. After I sent him a typed version of it, with the cheeky title *Desperately Seeking Enlightenment and Cheap Rugs*, Daniel made hundreds of photocopies, giving them out to anyone visiting Kullu. If it hadn't been for a telephone call months after we moved to Vancouver, I would never have known that a copy of it was circulating. The call came from a distraught father—from Nova Scotia, as it happened. He was worried about his daughter being pulled into the swami's orbit and wanted my opinion.

"What made you think I could possibly help with your daughter?" I asked him.

"I read your diary," he said.

Okey-dokey.

•   •   •

I could never have predicted the role my own father would play in my search for enlightenment. As I recorded in my diary, "Moments before yet another interview with the swami, cousin Daniel told me something I never knew, a conversation between his father and my mother, brother to sister. . . . Minutes before Mom went into the surgery that would kill her, she had unwrapped the bandages off her shaved head and my uncle kissed it. 'Why, Mennie?' she asked him. 'Why couldn't it just be appendicitis? Why brain surgery?' She must have known she was going to die. My uncle, hugging her, must have known too. They were knowers."

"It's showtime!" my cousin had said, smiling, after telling me that tender story of the final day of my mother's short life. But before the swami arrived for my final interview with him, I already *knew.* In a blinding moment of clarity, I could see precisely where my ability to keep moving came from. And I knew I would get through my next move home to Canada. I didn't credit the swami for any part of my enlightenment, at least not right away. As we set up the video camera, I knew exactly who I needed to thank for my ability not to unravel: my father. That came as a huge surprise to me. I hadn't been writing about him at all in my diary. I had been focused, as always, on my late mother.

Truth be told, my father hadn't exactly been the greatest role model. But there was one thing he did get right, and for that I remain grateful. He showed me what resilience looks like.

A week after the sudden loss of his wife of twenty years, my father donned his work clothes, packed a lunch for himself, and returned to his dental practice. He put one foot in front of the other and kept moving forward. He showed me how important it is to simply carry on with life. Of course, we mourned. Of course, we grieved. And of course, we would never forget my mother. But we didn't paralyze ourselves by focusing only on what we had lost or the unfairness of it all. Who said life was fair, anyway? My father showed me that life must be for the living.

But I also needed to give the swami his due. In his infinite, if convoluted, wisdom about the need to understand change through *unchange*, Swami Shyam taught me to focus on those parts of myself that had never changed and never would. That let me see the foundation of my being in a new light. My character wouldn't vanish in the jet stream as I flew across the Pacific from Korea to Canada. It would travel with me, always, down whichever road I chose to take.

A Smart-Ass
Fish Out of Water

"HELLO. THIS IS Robin Pascoe speaking. I'm a freelance journalist writing a story about people who ignore voice messages. Can you call me back, please?"

The world was shaken by a massive tectonic shift in the mid-1990s thanks to the arrival of e-mail. A hi-tech innovation embraced initially by computer geeks, e-mail began spreading to the masses after Hotmail created a free, use-anywhere internet e-mail service. Within a year, an estimated 10 million e-mailers had signed up for free webmail accounts. I was trying to build a new life in Vancouver just as the internet was becoming the hot new global destination.

Re-entry shock, an inescapable by-product of repatriation, can make anyone feel like an outsider in their own culture. But that didn't entirely explain my feelings of disengagement from my new neighbours. The breakdown of old social courtesies was the real culprit. New digital tools had made it possible (and, worse, socially acceptable) to stop talking to one another in real time. I was being *ghosted* long before the verb entered the lexicon.

The two books I had written for expatriate families were useless in my current, seemingly futile, search for meaningful work. No one cared about global living either—at least not yet.

Rodney, meanwhile, was off having the time of his life. His new job involved non-stop international business travel. I was left behind to settle in our young children and train our new border collie puppy, Cruise. While I lay prone on a couch listening to the incessant coastal rain, Cruise herded furniture around me and crapped all over the brightly coloured dhurrie rugs I had brought home from India. He was lucky he was so cute.

Then one day in the fall of 1996, I received an intriguing fax from the Singapore publisher of my two Culture Shock! titles. I had avoided communication with them since our return to Canada, other than to receive my royalty cheques, a dismal fifty cents on every book sold. Signing with the publisher before consulting someone who knew literary contracts had been a terrible idea. I had unwittingly surrendered the copyrights to both titles because I didn't know any better. Plus, I had blindly agreed to a 10 percent royalty rate, without understanding that the percentage was based not on the retail price but on the price the publisher sold the books for. With thousands of copies going at a heavily discounted price to distributors, the fifty-cent royalty I received might even have been on the high side.

That day, however, the publisher was forwarding a speaking invitation from an organization called Outpost that supported globally mobile families. They were having a conference on expat family matters—their first ever—the following spring at their headquarters in The Hague, and they wanted me to be the keynote speaker. "Would you happen to be in Europe at that time?" my publisher wanted to know. I couldn't stop laughing. Money was so tight at home that Rodney and I had a toonie jar to save up for caffe lattes. I could hardly afford to be swanning around Holland, even with all the air mile points my husband was racking up on his business travels. But then I read that all my expenses would be covered, from airfare to hotel.

After calling my Canadian friend Mary, who happened to be living in Holland, I discovered that Outpost worked on behalf of Royal Dutch Shell, the biggest employer of expats in the world. They had surveyed their families to learn what they needed in the way of relocation support, and it turned out my wife book was a highly recommended resource. Rodney felt guilty about all his own travel. The minute he told me to accept the invitation, I booked my flight to Holland.

•   •   •

"I don't know about you, ladies," I told my audience in The Hague the next spring, "but this repatriation business has been a nightmare for me. If I wasn't so tired and depressed, I'd write another book and devote it entirely to the challenges of moving home."

The response was swift. "*Please* write that book!" Many of the women there, a mixture of Brits and Dutch recently returned to home base, were suffering from their own re-entry shock, something no one had prepared them for. In one of the earliest forms of gaslighting I encountered, some wives were also being made to believe they must be crazy for feeling lousy. They were consistently told there were no repatriation challenges. Like me, they heard only *You're home now, what's the problem?*

The Shell conference lit a fire under me. As soon as I got back from Holland, I began writing *Homeward Bound: A Spouse's Guide to Repatriation*, the first of three new titles I would write and publish under my own imprint, Expatriate Press. New digital publishing platforms were springing up every day, and selling my own books at speaking engagements sounded like a perfect plan. I would also make significantly more than fifty cents per book. For the first time in almost a year, I felt motivated. I informed Rodney I was done with looking for a job. If I couldn't make enough money through my writing to help pay down our considerable mortgage, then I would try not to spend much. He would not have to support anything in my life, I promised him, except for hair colour four times a year, which was non-negotiable. There is only so much a girl is willing to give up for her art. And this time around, I would bow to the feminists and use "spouse" in the title, even though there was not a man alive who was going to read my book, never mind ask himself if menopause was making his repatriation worse.

In a serendipitous break, the first of many, I learned that Outpost had offices wherever the multinational Shell had families. Six months after speaking in The Hague, an e-mail popped up in my in-box with an invitation to speak from the Outpost office in Stavanger, a city of fjords considered the oil capital of Norway. Six months after that, Shell families living in Hong Kong invited me. My new career was launched. I would spend the next decade criss-crossing the globe, speaking about the challenges of mobility not just to oil families but also at international schools, women's clubs, expat community associations, and even chambers of commerce. There was no guidebook yet on this new way of working, since the term *digital nomad* was only just emerging. But I knew that to make it all work, I'd need to embrace the new technology myself. And quickly.

• • •

It was difficult to wrap my non-digital brain around the idea of a website. Fortunately, the long-suffering butt of my jokes and lectures came to the rescue. Rodney agreed to help me build it.

Like everything else associated with this new way of working, we made it up as we went along. We had one reference book: *HTML for Dummies*. I did all the coding and Rodney created the design, using the very limited choices available for fonts and colours. (Most homemade websites looked like neo-Nazi sites at that time, since unfortunately, the haters were also early adopters of the technology.) The day we successfully added a spinning globe to my homepage was a cause for celebration.

No one knew much about how to use a website either. What was it for, exactly? People were spending insane amounts of money to get websites built, only to have them serve as nothing more than static online brochures. I decided my site should reflect my values. That meant it had to be as much about giving stuff away as it was about selling something. I had plenty of content to offer for free: excerpts from my books, the numerous articles I was writing, chat groups anyone could join, and links to what other people were doing. I serialized an expat novel I'd written that had been rejected by publishers and created an Agony Aunt section inviting expat wives anywhere in the world to contact me and share their problems. I answered every e-mail and made many lifelong friends that way.

The DIY version of ExpatExpert.com went online in late 1998. Two years later, I hired a real web designer to create a more professional website. It featured the brilliant tagline he came up with: For Smart Fish Out of Water. A bespoke computer program called Expatomatic allowed me to post entries into a weblog. Before I took it offline fifteen years later, my site attracted hundreds of thousands of unique visitors a year from close to a hundred countries. I even faked my way through an appearance on a tech show, *CNNdotcom*, to discuss the importance of websites for expats. I had a good laugh over the first question the interviewer put to me: "Why do people living and moving overseas need a website?" Today, there are millions of websites devoted to people living and moving globally.

• • •

Perhaps nothing in my new digital life would prove as interesting as an appointment I made on a speaking visit to Amsterdam in the early aughts: I was going to have lunch with myself. Or at least with my Google doppelgänger. Part of the new craze of googling yourself was finding doppelgängers, or, as a *New Yorker* cartoon called them, googlegängers and doppelgoogles.

An e-mail had arrived in my in-box a few months earlier with the subject line: "Robin Pascoe needs to interview Robin Pascoe." It was from a British journalist trying to arrange an interview for a daily English-language financial newspaper in Amsterdam. I already knew there was someone with the same name as me working there, because she had co-authored a guidebook to the city. Her name came up with mine on Amazon.com.

Anyone taking notice of us over lunch in a little hole-in-the-wall restaurant near the central train station would have seen two middle-aged women laughing over coffee, pulling out reporters' notebooks at the exact same moment, and trying to hear each other over the clang of the multiple bracelets we both wore on our wrists. In conversation it turned out that we both claimed to be technophobes (ironic, since we had been introduced by our computers) and we had both spent a part of our lives living in Asia, she with a British military father.

Our similarities did end abruptly with our hair. Her Cornish ancestry bestowed upon her long, thick hair, straight and black, more than an ocean removed from my wild, curly, sort-of-blonde mop. It was clear we were related only by algorithm.

Fifteen years after our first encounter, we met again. I was in Holland to deliver the opening keynote for a conference hosted by an organization devoted to international families called Families in Global Transition. At the welcome reception the first evening, the "'other'" Robin Pascoe and I made a perfect photo for social media. With what we now know about the internet, our names will be linked forever.

Fear of Flying

IT'S LATE SUMMER, and my mother and I are travelling to Sydney, Nova Scotia. We are quite a dissimilar pair. An athletic, trim woman in her early forties, Bessie has dark hair and even darker eyes, a contrast to my dirty-blonde waves and hazel eyes. Clutching her hand, I walk across the apron towards a Trans-Canada Air Lines Viscount turboprop plane. But instead of the plane, my gaze is focused on the new party shoes I insisted on wearing that day along with my bright blue coat. A flight attendant, looking smart in her TCA uniform, stands at the top of a mobile steel staircase. I turn around for a final glance at the families on the outdoor observation deck, hoping to spot my father waving.

This is my earliest memory of air travel: Toronto International Airport, circa 1963. Within three years, the observation deck, symbolic of a more innocent time in air travel, would be gone. Malton Airport, as it was known then, would be replaced with a state-of-the-art circular terminal, and TCA would become Air Canada.

Every summer, my mother and I travelled to the island of Cape Breton, off Nova Scotia's eastern coast. "God's country," as one of my uncles called it, was where my mother had been born and raised. As the one appointed to accompany her on these annual visits with her parents, who lived in Glace Bay, I now count those trips as my happiest memories of her. Our flight that day was a milk run, landing multiple times along the way to our final destination. Our luggage contained precious cargo we would have hated to lose: several pounds of a sausage-like Jewish concoction known as *kishka* and enough kosher salamis to induce a serious sodium coma. These delicacies were available only at a certain delicatessen in Toronto, and my mother had been tasked with transporting them for guests attending the bar mitzvah of yet another of her nephews. Every summer there seemed to be a *simcha* to celebrate, since I had a great many cousins.

The summer of the *kishka*, I was ten years old and loved everything about flying. What kid didn't? Flying then was enormously special, worth dressing up for. Men wore suit jackets and ties. Women often wore corsages. It's hard to imagine such a thing now. Before tablets and mobile phones, a child had only her imagination for travel entertainment—and lots of books to read. The airline did provide a few distractions, though, like colouring kits and airline swag such as miniature plastic airplanes and pilot wings pins. The flight attendant offered candies to the adults, along with small packs of cigarettes. Given my mother's incessant puffing, we always sat in the smoking section. If we wanted to stretch our legs during one of the stops, we'd just plonk down the provided *Occupied* cards on our seats—reserved seating on airplanes wasn't yet a thing. Women even left their purses on their seats. For years, I collected those *Occupied* cards, until they too vanished.

Barely two years after that flight to Sydney, Bessie was dead. My Cape Breton grandmother suffered the double blow of losing her husband and her daughter in the space of two years. After that, she insisted on seeing me as often as possible, so I continued to make the journey to Cape Breton by prop plane. The difference was that I now flew alone.

In the same blink of an eye that had erased my mother, the colouring kits and toy airplanes were gone. By the time I was sixteen, I was the passenger smoking a cigarette and sipping a Dubonnet on the rocks with a twist of lemon, apparently an acceptable drink for an unaccompanied adolescent. (Different times, like I said.) As I stared out the window, my eyes welled up at the sight of the propellers spinning and grinding. My grief would roll down my face, and so began a lifelong habit of sobbing while flying. As a teenager, I should have been crying over an unrequited crush or a fight with a friend, not a dead mother. I wasn't the only flyer to get emotional—or morbid—at thirty-five thousand feet, though the aperitifs probably contributed. First out of curiosity, but later with mounting anxiety, I'd wonder, *What would happen if one of those props suddenly stopped?*

· · ·

Where does fear of flying come from, anyway? Some theories connect fear of flying to claustrophobia, others to a fear of heights. A few frightening incidents can trigger it—and I have had more than my fair share of those while flying in stormy weather.

When I was in my forties, I saw a hypnotherapist to try to deprogram my fears. After all, hypnosis had worked on my smoking habit: I would stop for months at a time, then years, and finally I managed to quit forever. I was hopeful that the power of suggestion would keep me calm in the air. The hypnotherapist first tried to determine the root of my anxiety. Together we reviewed a checklist of the various aspects of flying, including boarding, taxiing, and takeoff. Tick, tick, tick. They all sent me into a tailspin.

"And once you are in the air," he asked, "will you move around the cabin?"

"Well, a girl does have to pee," I replied. *Especially when she's been binge drinking.* I didn't say that last thought out loud: the hypnotherapist was aware of my strategy of self-medicating my anxiety on a plane.

"Do you mind turbulence?" he asked.

"Not really," I said, "unless the plane hits an air pocket and loses altitude." That had happened once, with oxygen masks falling down from overhead. This scared me and the other passengers, especially as few of us had paid attention to the instructions on how to use them.

"How about the landing? Are you afraid of that?" asked the hypnotherapist. "It's supposed to be the most dangerous part of the flight after the takeoff."

"Not afraid. I'm happy to be landing!"

"So just the takeoff, then?"

"Yes."

He considered my answers, wrote a few notes, and then pronounced, "You're not actually afraid of flying."

Huh?

"You just hate surrendering control to the pilot. It's not uncommon. And, of course, you do fear a sudden, catastrophic incident. That's really at the heart of it."

Ah yes, fear of sudden death.

. . .

My fear of flying only worsened once I had children. What if something happened to me and they too became motherless? This paranoia, I should point out, is not restricted to daughters who have lost their mothers. The thought surely crosses every parent's mind when their plane lifts into the sky. Clearly, I had to manage my anxiety: as the wife of a diplomat and later in my work as the globe-trotting "Expat Expert," I could not avoid flying. Unfortunately, the hypnosis hadn't worked, though even today I think of the actor Kevin Costner at every takeoff: my hypnotherapist had suggested I think of something or someone to distract myself.

Alcohol worked like a charm to calm me down. I had graduated from the Dubonnet on the rocks of my teenage years to drinking straight vodka. It was better than scotch for flying purposes because it didn't smell as strong. At first, a few rapid shots at the airport bar would set me up for a flight. But after losing track of time once too often, I knew I needed a better system. It wasn't hard to devise one back then, before carrying liquids onto an airplane was considered a potential act of terrorism. As part of my packing ritual, I would empty most of a small bottle of orange juice and replace the juice with vodka, icy cold from my freezer. What juice there was left in the bottle made the contents appear to be what the label claimed it was: 100 percent orange juice. By my best estimate, the bottle held between six and eight one-and-a-half-ounce shots of vodka. If I drank it quickly, that was certainly enough to knock me out, as long as alcohol poisoning didn't kill me first.

After much trial and error, I had figured out the best time to begin drinking my pre-flight cocktail: the moment the plane pushed back from the gate. The taxiing gave me enough time to get drunk before the plane was in position, ready to accelerate down the runway. And no one suspected a thing. But occasionally, I didn't have the chance to mix my "cocktail" or hit an airport bar before a flight. One of the times that I boarded sober turned out to be the most important milestone in my career as the Expat Expert. I was scheduled to speak in the UK, as I frequently did during the early 2000s. I managed to give a talk at many of the international schools in and around London in those years. Not only did I love speaking to expats in London, the trips gave me the opportunity to see a West End musical. And I loved how straightforward it was to get to London from Vancouver: one non-stop flight to Heathrow. True, it was a ten-hour flight, but a good book usually carried me through.

On this particular day, returning home from a speaking trip, I had time to browse the bookstore at Heathrow but not time to booze up. Boarding without any vodka in my system, I felt a bit jangled. Seating myself on the aisle, I smiled at the man sitting next to me. As usual, the flight was packed. Besides takeoff, I also found boarding to be unnerving. I would carefully survey everyone walking down the aisle as if I were an air marshal. Even a small commotion could upset me, and that day was no exception. As people struggled to get their luggage into the overhead bins, I started to feel anxious and also angry—at myself, mostly, for being sober.

Eventually, once all the bags were stowed and the passengers seated, the pilot pushed back from the gate and the plane started to make its way to the runway for takeoff. The weather was not pleasant, and the dark clouds looked threatening. I knew it would be a bumpy climb skyward. Of course, the turbulence began the moment I thought about it. I grabbed the arm of the kind-looking man beside me. "I am so sorry," I said, worrying that I was actually going to harm him with my death grip. "I'm afraid I don't have any vodka in me," I told him, as if he would understand what I was talking about. "I'll be fine when we reach cruising altitude and I can get a drink."

"It's okay," he said, bemused. Perhaps this was not the first time a frantic seatmate had grabbed his arm and held on for dear life.

"I'm—serious—really," I stammered. I rang the bell for the flight attendant the moment the seatbelt sign was turned off and begged for a drink.

Manners dictated I chat with this poor man who'd had the bad luck to sit next to me, so once I had let the vodka do its work, I asked him the million-dollar question: "What do you do?"

"I'm a mover," he replied.

"A mover? Like—" and I named a moving company as an example.

"Yes, only we're Canadian. What do you do?"

"Well, as it happens, I write books for families who move."

We marvelled at the coincidence and exchanged business cards while I explained that I was returning to Vancouver after lecturing about my books in London. For good measure, I also threw in the fact that I rarely spoke in Canada and had little support in my own country—not from the foreign service my husband and I had once been part of, nor from multinational businesses. Not even travel bookstores carried my books for expats, which they considered too specialized. I made sales either through Amazon or at the back of the lecture halls where I spoke.

"I'll look you up in Canada," said the nice man who hadn't minded having his arm mangled.

After that, I didn't bother him for the rest of the flight. I dozed off after several more vodkas and never gave him another thought. Until six months later when, out of the blue, he phoned me.

"We would like to have you speak to our executive committee next month here in Vancouver. You can bring your books."

What a treat for me to load up the trunk of my car and drive downtown instead of to the airport. Not only did I enjoy meeting and presenting to the company executives, but I walked out with their commitment to sponsor my website, buy hundreds of my books, and have me travel under their banner in a few months' time to Bangkok and Manila to speak to their clients—a trip that would coincide with the launch of my fourth title, *A Moveable Marriage*. The company, AMJ Campbell International, would pay for everything and ship my books too. I thought I was dreaming. I wasn't.

Grabbing hold of serendipity was a delightful unintended consequence of my fear of flying. But even when I fly today, I can still be caught staring out the window, pulling out my sunglasses along with a tissue or two from my bag. Some old habits never die.

On the Book Tour Trail

RIGHT FROM THE start, my career as an author bore little resemblance to the way Hollywood portrays a writer's life. The publication of my first Culture Shock! title perfectly captured the gap between an aspirational movie narrative and reality: there were no fancy receptions, media interviews, or overnight fame. That may happen on the silver screen, but I was nowhere near Tinseltown. I was living in China.

Rodney was first secretary then in the political section at the Canadian embassy in Beijing. Despite his best efforts to pull diplomatic levers, several hundred copies of *The Wife's Guide to Successful Living Abroad* remained stuck in bureaucratic hell after being shipped from Singapore, where they were published. When they were finally released from Chinese customs, we celebrated in the garden clubhouse of our embassy, where I signed copies for a small group of friends. Afterwards, a few beers were hoisted in my honour before we jumped on our bikes to grab cheeseburgers at Frank's, a popular expat eatery in Beijing. The launch of my debut book had been as anticlimactic and low-key as Rodney's marriage proposal in Winnipeg. Both were life-altering events and were nothing like those portrayed by Hollywood.

It was from Beijing, however, that I set out on my first book tour. I probably wouldn't have done a promotional trip at all if

Rodney hadn't pushed me out the door.

"Go—by—myself?" I stuttered when he suggested I travel in the region. Frankly, I was terrified. "Where would I even begin? How would I plan it?" In the movies, there were always publicity teams lining everything up.

"You have good friends in Tokyo, Hong Kong, and Singapore," he pointed out, giving me the three large expat communities within striking range. "Fax everyone you know in those cities. Tell them you want to come and speak about your book. They will help you." Rodney was right. They did. In the process, an operational template was created for my book tours in the fifteen years to follow. Fax friends (later, e-mail), throw out a net to expat community organizations, lecture, sell books at the back of the room. Repeat.

Even after I partnered with Canadian mover AMJ Campbell International, I still relied on the kindness and generosity of my expat girlfriends. Other accompanying wives were my best publicists and cheerleaders. They understood the value of what I had written. And they were incredibly professional. One of my partners in crime was the British writer, publisher, and expat author Jo Parfitt. Together, referring to ourselves as The JoRo Show, we went on the road. Between the time we met at a conference in Paris in 1998 and 2010, when we were jointly honoured by Families in Global Transition for being "trailblazers," we spoke together in the UK, Switzerland, Italy, Holland, Germany, Luxembourg, and even the United States. Other friends lined up multiple events for me, from London to Santiago to Shanghai and many places in between. I was grateful to every one of them.

And it was a good thing I had all the help. When my first book came out in 1992, the Singapore publisher offered nothing except an invitation for lunch if I ever made it to their city (which I did on that first tour, and they did indeed take me for a nice lunch at the Tanglin Club). To be fair, there isn't an author alive who feels her publisher is doing enough marketing for her. I made the right decision in 2000 when I created my own imprint.

I learned a valuable lesson about the book trade from my first tour: it was up to me, the author, to drive the sales of my book. And that was especially true after I became a self-publisher. Travelling by myself, though, was not without its perils, and some journeys were particularly fraught.

Houston, we have a problem (2001)

Given my earlier experience speaking to oil families, Houston was a logical place to promote *Homeward Bound*, my book about reverse culture shock and repatriation. It was also my first self-published title, and I was still learning the ropes.

Finding speaking engagements in Houston was easy. Getting there proved less so, even before 9/11 changed air travel forever. Border controls between Canada and the United States, two countries with the longest peaceful border in the world, were less daunting than overseas ones, and pre-clearance protocols in major Canadian airports were also less complicated. What never changes, though, are the American bubbas behind passport control desks. (For the record, Canucks at the border can be hard-asses too. What is it about people in uniform with guns? Do they all love nothing better than to intimidate whoever stands before them presenting a passport? That behaviour seems to be universal.) I also have a distinct pathology that is not helpful at border crossings. I cannot lie to authority figures or to anyone else, for that matter. I don't dissemble well. Call it a character flaw.

As I set out one morning in early January 2001, ready to launch my US book marketing offensive, I stepped up to the podium at Vancouver International Airport, handing over my passport to US customs for pre-clearance. Within seconds, I was cut at the knees.

"Are you being paid to speak in Houston?" asked the American border official, a humourless bald man I still see in my nightmares.

As usual, I told the truth. "I'm receiving an honorarium of $500."

"Please move over there, ma'am," he ordered me, avoiding eye contact.

"Oh? My plane leaves in forty-five minutes. How long will I be waiting over there?"

"Please move over there, ma'am," he repeated, motioning to the next traveller to step up.

I was kept waiting long enough to miss my flight. Even after an hour, I still didn't know what the holdup was about. Finally, I was asked to sit down for a chat with another official, who informed me I was being denied entry into the United States of America that day. When I asked why, he said he was not allowed to tell me.

I called Rodney, crying with frustration. He magically appeared within the hour. Since this happened before post-9/11 barricades went up, he managed to get into the "back area" at the airport and found me sitting on a bench, sobbing. He too tried to get some answers from the officials. They were having none of it.

Apparently there was something every Canadian travelling to the United States on business knew except me. I had slept through the news of the North American Free Trade Agreement in the 1980s, but I had an excuse. That was the decade I was busy having babies. If I had paid better attention, I would have known it was okay to claim a payment if you had a special visa, had won the Nobel Prize, or were Mother Theresa. Ordinary schleppers like me just missed their flights. In the future, I would devise a work-around when speaking in the States. Advance book sales and travel expenses meant I didn't have to lie about being paid a speaking fee.

Rodney placed the call to my hosts in Texas. "Houston, we have a problem," he announced into his phone as we were walking back to the airport parking lot. At least that gave me a good laugh. It was better than crying.

The Reichstag, Berlin (2004)

On March 8, 2004, Todd Bertuzzi, a player for my hometown hockey team, the Vancouver Canucks, skated up the ice after an opponent, grabbed his jersey, and punched him in the side of the head. In the ensuing dog pile, the other player suffered three fractured vertebrae, facial cuts, and a concussion. He would never play hockey again.

I learned of this brutal hit in the lobby of the Intercontinental Hotel in Berlin, where I was staying with my girlfriend Mary. The story blared from more than one television. In the days before social media and smartphones, breaking news was delivered the old-fashioned way. The more amplified versions of news delivery, Twitter et al., had not yet been invented. That was lucky for me, since I could have been crucified, or at the very least cancelled, if an offhand, ill-considered offensive comment I had made during my lecture in Berlin had gone viral. In a daze of jet lag, I had completely forgotten who was in my audience.

I was in Berlin at the invitation of the family support organization for German diplomats. Since they had alerted others in the diplomatic community, the turnout for my event was very good. The venue was a lecture hall in the historic German government building, the Reichstag. To say the surroundings were intimidating to a Jewish woman would be understating how I felt. Looking back, I blame the Holocaust loop running through my head as I looked around a room in which Hitler may have stood. Still, there was no excuse for the exchange that took place after my lecture was finished and we had moved on to the question-and-answer period.

"I'm X and my husband is Y and we are living in Z," a young mother asked. "How do we raise our children given this number of competing cultures?"

"I'm so glad you asked that," I began, explaining that the subject of cross-cultural marriages always came up at my lectures. "I do understand the challenges of mixed marriages," I continued, smiling. "I also happen to be in one. I'm Jewish and my husband isn't. And when we decided to get married, both our fathers wanted to put their heads in an oven because they were so upset."

Jews? Oven? In the same sentence? In the German Reichstag? *Oy vey!*

I looked over at Mary, sitting at my book sales table. She could barely control her laughter. I quickly brought the proceedings to a close with a pitch to buy my books, which I would, of course, be happy to sign. As some folks headed for the books table, others for the door, Mary jumped up to chase after a tall, striking blonde woman who had just nicked a copy of one of my books and dropped it into her purse without paying. Mary never managed to catch up with her.

I wasn't the least bit surprised by what had happened at the books table. There were always a few women who helped themselves to my books after I'd given a talk, sometimes one copy, sometimes more. That day, at least, the petty thievery provided a welcome distraction from my gaffe.

India (2008)

At the Novotel in Hyderabad, I sat unnoticed in the grand lobby in my pyjamas with a borrowed hotel laptop, checking my e-mail, drinking coffee, and chain-smoking at 6:00 a.m. Hyderabad was the fourth stop on my five-city speaking tour of India, which had been arranged by a partner of my Canadian movers, Santa Fe Relocation. I had already lectured in Delhi, Bangalore, and Chennai, and my body was feeling it. Badly. Indian food, to be polite, was not agreeing with me. I had been reduced to living on the granola bars and peanut butter I had brought with me.

Directly in my line of sight stood an embarrassing giant cut-out of myself, advertising the lectures I was to give in the convention centre next door to the hotel. I had asked to have the cut-out removed the previous evening after spotting it during check-in, but there it still was, looking defiantly back at me. Luckily, no one spotting me parked on the oversized couch in my bathrobe would have made the connection between the two images. There was much more interesting stuff to watch in the hotel's lobby, even at that early hour.

Several large wedding parties with hundreds of guests in brightly coloured attire had already blown through the lobby at some designated auspicious time. They were out the door so quickly, I wondered if I had been hallucinating from dehydration. Uniformed "sprayers" also roamed the lobby, deploying giant cans of highly toxic Deet to fight the mosquitoes. I puffed away and read my e-mail, wondering how I could possibly be lecturing in such a place.

When I finally spoke later that morning, it was the first time in my career I had to excuse myself from the podium to make a mad dash for the bathroom. The audience was understanding, of course. They were living in India, right? They knew the drill. I only wish I had been as sympathetic with some of them. Cranky due to my case of the runs, I lost my cool with a mother who asked a reasonable question about disciplining her son during the sensitive time of transition to a new place, especially one as overwhelming as India. Her son, this mom told us, had asked for a tech toy, a PlayStation, and assured his mom that the toy would make him feel better.

Kids weren't stupid, I always told parents. They knew full well when a parent, especially a mom, was feeling guilty about a relocation and would take the opportunity to pounce. That morning, though, I practically shouted my answer.

"Are you crazy? Can't you see he's trying to manipulate you?

Moving your child doesn't mean you have to deliver non-stop happiness. Just say no!"

I stopped short, mortified by my outburst. I prided myself on smiling during these occasions, no matter what. Travelling around the world to lecture was more than a job. It was a gift. Afterwards, when I saw the poor mother I had harangued approaching the books table, I jumped up. Everyone thought I was running again to the bathroom, so they cleared a path for me. But I was heading at full speed for the mom, so I could take her hand in mine and apologize.

"No need," she said. "I wanted to thank *you*."

Wait, what?

"Parents don't get enough realistic advice. I needed to hear what you had to say. We all did."

By the time I reached Mumbai, the final stop on my tour, I was running on fumes and hard-boiled eggs, since my stash of granola bars had run out. Rodney was also in India on business, and we had arranged to meet in Mumbai once my tour was over.

While in India, I had been accompanied by a "handler" appointed by my hosts. Thanks to Monica, I hadn't been swept away in a sea of humanity on arrival in airports in Chennai, Bangalore, Hyderabad, or Mumbai, all since upgraded to shiny new terminals but still the stuff of nightmares back then. Simply reading the list of prohibited carry-on items—from radioactive material, nunchakus (Indian fighting sticks), and cricket bats to guns, knives, and explosives—was almost paralyzing for someone like me with a profound fear of flying.

Once we got to Mumbai, Monica left me to return home to her family in Delhi. We said our goodbyes after a quick bite in the hotel lounge, where we noticed that the other guests looked a bit, to be kind, unsavoury. Returning to my room, I discovered that the door did not lock. I dragged over furniture to block the door from any intruder before falling onto the bed, exhausted. Then came the next surprise. The lights would not turn off. Grabbing my airplane mask to shut out the light, I slept fitfully and awakened long before dawn. I crawled to the lobby, again in my pyjamas, to use a public computer I had noticed the night before. I figured no one else would be down there so early.

I was immersed in my webmail when the lobby guard approached me.

"Madam, there is a telephone call for you."

"Are you sure?" How could he possibly know there was a call for me, especially this early? I didn't remember announcing my name.

I picked up the receiver. Rodney was on the other end.

"How on earth did you track me down?"

"No one answered when they rang your room," he said. "So I called the reception desk and asked if there was a wild-looking white woman with curly hair chain-smoking in her bathrobe on a computer anywhere in the lobby."

"Come get me!" And he did.

Travel Karma

Once there was a Chinese farmer whose horse ran away. That evening, all of his neighbours came around to commiserate. They said, "We are so sorry to hear your horse has run away. This is most unfortunate."

The farmer said, "Maybe."

The next day the horse came back, bringing seven wild horses with it, and in the evening everybody came back and said, "Oh, isn't that lucky. What a great turn of events. You now have eight horses!"

The farmer again said, "Maybe."

The following day his son tried to break one of the horses, and while riding it, he was thrown and broke his leg. The neighbours then said, "Oh dear, that's too bad," and the farmer responded, "Maybe."

The next day the conscription officers came to draft people into the army, and they rejected the farmer's son because he had a broken leg. Again all the neighbours said, "Isn't that great!"

Again, the farmer said, "Maybe."

—The Old Man Who Lost His Horse, ancient Chinese proverb

WHENEVER THEIR FATHER launches into that famous Taoist parable on silver linings, my children (now adults) roll their eyes. But there's a reason Rodney repeats it often. It's an excellent reminder that a setback in life one day may turn out to be a blessing the next. And so it can be for the traveller. A trip goes sideways (a cancelled flight due to stormy weather, perhaps) and a wonderful adventure is the unforeseen consequence. For this particular traveller, thanks to making a presentation after a brouhaha (involving the police) in Lausanne, Switzerland, I found myself, barely a year later, on a private safari near Kruger National Park, in South Africa.

It was the fall of 2003, the year I published *A Moveable Marriage*. I was in Lausanne to promote my book at a conference and had arrived on Kol Nidre, the holiest night of the Jewish High Holidays. I wouldn't be joining any congregants for prayers that evening, however, or fasting, as was the custom. Instead, I was hanging with my other tribe, the professional women I worked with on all matters related to families and global living. We had gathered in Switzerland for an annual networking event, the successful brainchild of a Norwegian woman. With its beautiful conference centre and tourism infrastructure, Lausanne provided the perfect venue—except for one small matter. The Swiss are a very rules-oriented society. One of their regulations concerns bus tickets. Riders must purchase one *before* boarding a bus, using the machines set up at every bus stop.

Sounds easy enough, unless you're a group of a dozen women returning to their hotel in high spirits after enjoying dinner and drinking way too much wine. The conference didn't officially begin until the next day, but we were getting a head start on our networking. Aware of the rules, we all had exact change for our fares at the ready in our pockets. Our bus was pulling away from the bus stop, however, when the driver spotted us running to catch it. He stopped, allowing us to hop on board. We tried to give him our money, but he waved us off. *What a friendly place*, we thought. Barely two blocks later, the bus pulled over and we were escorted off by transit police officers for riding illegally, without tickets. The driver had apparently reported us. So much for being friendly.

A French speaker among us tried to explain the misunderstanding, pointing out that we were visitors to Lausanne, not a group of locals trying to flout the rules. We again tried to pay for our tickets, but our gesture had no effect. Two more official vehicles appeared on the scene, only these new arrivals were real Swiss police officers. It must have been a slow night at the cop shop if a dozen foreign women, in town for a conference and allegedly trying to catch a free ride on a bus, were making the police radio.

As the squad cars pulled up, my friend Mary said: "Oh, good. The police are here now. They'll get this sorted out."

That wasn't what happened. One aggressive cop came and stood very close to me. Claiming we now owed a hefty fine for our transgression, he announced it must be paid on the spot. In cash. It was hard not to believe that this was an off-the-books shakedown. We explained, calmly, that even if we wanted to pay this suspicious fine (cash? really? with no official ticket issued to us?), we didn't have any money on us, having just spent it on dinner. As a gentle drizzle began to fall, our collective good mood evaporated. The air held a chill. We could secure the money, we offered, if the police could just follow us to our hotel.

"No," the aggressive cop said. "We will take *this* one to the hotel to get the money. The rest of you, wait here."

Guess who he chose? As this nasty fellow loaded me into the back seat of his patrol car, I frantically called over to Mary to please come join me. Never separate from the pack: every woman knows this rule.

"*No!* Just this one," the officer barked. Then he mimicked the way I had called out to her, turning the chill I was feeling into a full-body cold panic. He was a bully. By now it was late at night, in a European city where the sirens we could hear in the distance echoed the distinct sound they make in too many World War II movies. All I could think was *Sure, pick the only Jew in the group, on Yom Kippur, no less.* I struggled not to let my mind transport me somewhere evil.

I had no choice but to go with the police officer to our hotel. My friends told me later I looked like the proverbial deer caught in the headlights. I was worried at first that the police were taking me somewhere else. In short order, though, I was back with the group, carrying the cash I had quickly emptied out of my hotel safe—enough to cover everyone's transit fines. Our hotel manager returned with me to the scene of the so-called crime. She tried to help us resolve the situation, but to no avail. Afterward, we all retreated to her establishment, where she offered us a good stiff drink. I lay awake and shaking the entire night.

The matter did not end there. After we complained to the organizers of the conference the following day, a meeting was quickly arranged by Tourism Lausanne. It didn't help their image that a dozen international women, many of us journalists, had been caught up in unnecessary foolishness. The transit police officer who had started it all was brought in to apologize to us, which he did, sort of, and he grudgingly returned our money. The police commissioner also offered an official apology before presenting us with Swiss chocolates. Like that was going to solve matters. Not a chance.

Lausanne was a brief weekend stopover on my promotional book tour. I had already spoken in the Netherlands (which was why I had cash from book sales in my hotel safe), but I was scheduled to continue on to Dusseldorf and Frankfurt. I'd planned to take a train from Geneva to Germany, to chill out after the conference on my own. But relaxing was now out of the question.

My friends and colleagues almost unanimously suggested that I call off the rest of my tour and head home to Vancouver. But Mary, my best friend and conscience, reminded me of the disappointment that would ensue if my plans were cancelled. If I ran away, she said, I would be reneging on my commitments. Worse, I would be capitulating to a bully. She was right. Reluctantly, I boarded a train to Germany. Rather than relax and look out the window at the scenery, though, I spent the entire ten-hour journey checking and rechecking my ticket. I would later have to deal with my PTSD in therapy. All over a silly bus ticket.

•   •   •

Early the following year, I received a phone call from Geneva. A manager with a global company that helps businesses with their human resources needs, including global relocations, was calling to invite me to speak at a conference in Paris in May.

"We'd like you to talk about your new marriage book," he

said. "My wife heard you speak about it at a women's conference in Lausanne last fall."

I could hardly believe it. Not only that his wife had been at the conference, but that she had recommended me. I'd been zombie-like during my presentation, still processing our bullying by the cops. But now here was her husband, tracking me down to ask me to speak at a conference. In Paris, in the springtime! I felt a bit like the Old Woman Who Didn't Pay Her Bus Ticket, and then remembered how the Chinese proverb had unfolded. Travelling to Paris would be fantastic. *Maybe.*

The invitation was for the kind of speaking engagement I had started to loathe. I didn't consider human resources to be "my people"; they were more like adversaries who had to be convinced it was worth spending money to support the relocating global family. For every enlightened soul I met from the corporate world—and obviously the man inviting me would fall into that category—there were too many who simply didn't understand spousal concerns. I braced myself beforehand for an unpleasant interaction with some of the participants, and that's precisely what transpired.

After my keynote address about the stresses in expat marriages—during which I outlined a thousand and one ways that marriage challenges can impact an assignment—the first question I got was this one: "Robin, why do we need to even be speaking about marriage in international relocations?"

Sigh. I tried to remain polite. "I never realized that *all* of your employees on international assignments were single."

"No," this gentleman responded. "Many of our employees are married."

"That's why we need to discuss marriage. Next question, please."

The room was silent, but only briefly. As most public speakers can attest, there is always someone in the audience who loves the sound of their own voice. On this day, it was a woman from a Russian oil company. She disputed everything I had said in my speech and threw in a few disrespectful jabs at me.

"You don't know what you're talking about," she said. "Our spouses are all *very* happy. You would know this if you ever spoke to *important* women's groups such as"—and here she mentioned an international group in Geneva, clearly the centre of her universe. So she was a snob too. Wonderful. The man sitting next to her couldn't resist throwing more oil on the fire. "Pretty much everything you have said is misinformed," he pronounced.

I'm not proud to admit this, but at that point I completely lost my cool. Shaking with righteous indignation, I listed off my considerable bona fides. When my host politely closed out the session, I left the conference room quickly and headed straight to the hotel bar. I pulled out the picture of my children I always carried in my purse and propped it up on the table, using it to focus on what was really important in my life. I was on my way to getting plastered, and chain-smoking too, when two men, Afrikaners from Johannesburg who were attending the conference, spotted me. They wasted no time in coming directly over.

"That pair were complete jackasses," one of them said by way of hello. I loved him immediately. The other gushed about my Culture Shock! books. His company had been using them with clients for years, he said. The men were partners in an

HR consultancy that worked with expats, a growing field in post-apartheid South Africa. There had been an explosion in expat assignments there, both coming and going, after Nelson Mandela became president.

"Too bad you never get to South Africa," one of them said.

"Who says I never get there?" I asked them. "Why don't you invite me?"

And so they did, even making promises to take me on a safari. We sat drinking and smoking until closing time in that Paris bar. Which may explain why I didn't come to my senses that night, to tell them I was petrified of wild animals and couldn't go on safari. Six months later, I boarded a flight in Vancouver and headed for the first leg of a trip to Johannesburg. I hoped that upon landing in South Africa, I would remember what the two men looked like. As my cousin Nancy had rightly asked me before I left, "Do you even know these guys, Robin?"

"Not really," I told her. "But they seemed nice. And they plan to take me on a private safari! How fabulous is that going to be?" *Maybe.*

• • •

After two full days and nights of flying to get there, I was relieved to recognize one of my hosts standing in the arrivals hall, holding flowers for me. *Phew.* He didn't live in Johannesburg proper but on a small holding in a nearby rural suburb called Krugersdorp. I hadn't realized I would be staying *on a farm in Africa* and immediately channelled my inner Karen Blixen, or at least the voice of Meryl Streep, who played her in the movie *Out of Africa*. On my first evening there, I sat outside with my host and his family, dazzled by an orange sunset over a savannah that stretched as far as the eye could see.

Before leaving Canada, I had learned a bit more about the three-day safari scheduled to happen after my speaking engagement. It had been the source of much discussion with Rodney, mostly because of that matter of my fear of animals. He and our daughter Lilly had been on a safari together a few years earlier in Botswana. I had seen their pictures and heard all their stories. From these, I thought I had some idea of what lay in store for me. I could not have been more wrong.

Far from anything organized by a tour company, it turned out our trip would involve us staying at a camp in a private game reserve called Klaserie, adjacent to the world-famous Kruger National Park. By "us," I mean me and my four companions on this adventure: my two hosts, both men in their early forties (ten years younger than I was), and two sixteen-year-old youths, the son of one of my hosts and his buddy. I would be the lone woman. They had already decided the sixteen-year-old son would be the designated driver of the Land Rover on our rides out in the morning to see the wildlife and in the evenings to the bush pub. That way, his elders could drink. And drink. And drink. On that score, I had absolutely no objections.

Before leaving Krugersdorp, I called or e-mailed everyone important in my life to say goodbye. A bit over-the-top, perhaps, but it made me feel better. Then, with my host's truck loaded up with every conceivable food and drink item we could possibly need on our adventure, we hit the road. It was a seven-hour drive between Johannesburg and Kruger. We drove through miles and miles of plains, eventually reaching rugged mountain landscapes.

We did a cultural exchange of tunes along the way. I had brought a Michael Bublé CD to introduce the Vancouver crooner who would end up a global phenomenon. My host turned me on to the music of Afrikaner singer-songwriter Karen Zoid, a South African diplomat's daughter whose career as a rock star was just taking off. There were long stretches of road with nowhere a middle-aged woman with an active bladder could stop, but that didn't matter. I had discovered *biltong*, salty strips of dried meat that curbed my urge to pee. *Biltong* was like crack cocaine for a sodium nut like me. I devoured pounds of it. Later, when I found out I wouldn't be able to relieve myself without being accompanied by one of my travel companions, carrying a rifle, I thought about eating *biltong* all night long too.

A flat tire delayed us, meaning we arrived at the camp as the sun was setting. There was just enough light for one of the youths to spot—and, thankfully, trap—a poisonous green mamba snake that was crawling up a tree alongside the platform, built on stilts, that we would all be sleeping on together, side by side. The corrugated tin roof over the platform would be a source of considerable stress and agitation for me on our final night, when thunder and lightning (a "proper African storm," as one of my hosts explained) threatened to incinerate us. Below the platform was an open-air space my hosts told me was for wandering lions who happened to break through the brick wall surrounding the camp. They showed me where the wall had been rebuilt after one such incident. Vaguely I heard something about sleeping and bathing in our clothes, but I was already asking for a drink. Please.

We spent that first night sitting around a campfire made with slow-burning *hardekool*, the South African lead wood that gives off intense heat, used for cooking and apparently keeping wild animals at bay. The smell of the chicken roasting over the fire still attracted hyenas, but by the time they surrounded us, I had consumed so much alcohol I barely noticed. In the morning, I awakened blind. At least, momentarily. Luckily, my host, who was lying next to me with a rifle, waiting politely for me to awaken, instantly reassured me. "Don't worry, Robin. It's just the smoke from the *hardekool* fire. I forgot to warn you about it. Your eyes will clear in a minute or two." My vision was restored in time to focus on our morning drink, vodka and orange juice. I sucked it back before we headed to the Land Rover for our first morning ride.

And so began my time on a most unusual safari. There were forays each morning to see animals roaming freely. After lunch, which was usually around four, we showered in cold water and lay around letting the breeze dry our wet clothes. In the distance, from the living quarters of the workers in the park, came the sound of transistor radios broadcasting a soccer game. The men would nap while I scribbled in my diary. One day, the boys taught me how to fire a rifle, the first and only time in my life I have held a firearm. My shoulder was sore for weeks afterwards, though I did manage to hit one of the cans they had set up for me in a makeshift firing range. When I did want to bathe without my clothes on, my host stood close to the outdoor shower stall, half-naked himself from the heat, rifle over his shoulder.

Our drives in the evenings to the bush pub, just as the bright orange African sun was setting, were awe-inspiring. One night, as we were returning, the jeep broke down in the pitch dark. The four men with me all pulled out their rifles immediately as I saw my life flash before my eyes. Miraculously, there was cell coverage. I had no idea who my host was speaking to (who does one call to be rescued in the middle of nowhere?) until he passed me his phone. Before handing it over, he said to whoever it was, "You will never guess who is with us at the moment!"

"I knew it could only be you," said a voice on the other end of the phone. It belonged to none other than the lovely man from Geneva whose wife had heard me speak in Lausanne and who had later invited me to speak in Paris. My South African friends couldn't resist calling him, to share that I was with them and to pass the time chatting until the boys managed to get the Land Rover moving again.

On my final night in South Africa, my hosts took me to one of their favourite spots, which offered a glorious, panoramic view of both Klaserie and Kruger National Park.

"Everything becomes holy and comes to rest," offered one of the men I had started referring to as my old lions, to distinguish them from the youths. We were solemnly surveying the extraordinary scene of setting sun and bush. Then, out of the corner of my eye, I saw something move.

"Get in the car now!" one of the old lions said, indicating some real ones nearby.

"Sit and finish your scotch, Robin," advised the other old lion.

Remarkably, I lingered for a few moments, marvelling at how unafraid I was. Then I hightailed it to the Land Rover. I wasn't going to push my luck. But while the sun was ebbing as we made our way back to camp, I couldn't help but wonder. Could my Klaserie experience bring to an end my anxiety about wild animals, lightning strikes, and poisonous snakes? *Maybe.*

A Tribe Was Born

ONE AUTUMN EVENING in the mid-aughts, I was speaking to expatriate parents at the American School of London about my latest book, *Raising Global Nomads*. The event was in the school library and it was packed, which is always gratifying. There were even a few teenagers in the audience. As I was signing copies of my books afterwards, one of the teens approached me.

"Are you a mind reader or something?" the young girl asked me. "You must have moved around a lot when you were a child. You really seem to *get it*."

"Actually, I lived in Toronto my entire childhood," I said. But her question got me thinking. "When I was about your age, I made a move I had no control over. Maybe that's why I understand how you feel." It was true. Until that evening, though, I had never connected the dots.

When I was sixteen, my father remarried. Herb was barely fifty and had been a widower for four long years. No one expected him to be alone forever. Even I had encouraged him to start dating again. The timing of his nuptials, though, couldn't have been worse for me. I was halfway through grade twelve. Ontario still had grade thirteen back then, so before I could possibly escape to college, I had another eighteen months of high school ahead of me.

Michael and Laurie, my older brothers, left home within months of the wedding. Now that our father was settled again, it made perfect sense for them to get on with their lives and education. Michael was finishing medical school at the University of Toronto, and Laurie was moving down east to study commerce at Dalhousie before applying to law school there. I resented my brothers. Their departures meant I was left on my own to deal with our father and his new wife, Shirley. My new stepsister Susie, with whom I would eventually be very close, still lived at home with her mother. However, she had recently become engaged, so was occupied with her wedding plans.

My new stepmother was a highly opinionated woman with a laser-like focus on changing me, from the clothes I wore to the friends I made. As a team, Herb and Shirley set about making radical changes that created fresh losses in my life. With my brothers out of the picture and my father preoccupied, this time the losses were mine alone to deal with.

Our modest North Toronto family home went on the market right away. With its sale went all my cherished memories of my mother still alive: standing in our kitchen making dinner; wrapped in a blanket on the couch in our den, reading a library book; or just sitting in our breakfast nook, on the phone with one of her many sisters-in-law, her coffee cup and ashtray close at hand. My father had ignored all advice to buy a brand new residence for a fresh start. Instead, we moved into Shirley's place. Our family mementos and pictures were placed in boxes for removal, even my brothers' framed bar mitzvah portraits. The second Mrs. Pascoe didn't want any trace of the first one in her designer-decorated home.

Next to go was my school and the instrumental music program that was my passion. (I played the flute in a concert band, piccolo in a marching band, and percussion in an orchestra. There were rehearsals most days after school.) Just as grade thirteen was about to begin, I was told I would be attending a private girls' school in Toronto. Who gets parachuted into another school for their final year, never mind a private school, and so soon after a second marriage? What were they thinking?

There were intangible losses too. My late mother, who came from a small coal-mining town in Nova Scotia, had instilled in me virtues like humility and generosity. She role-modelled volunteerism with her work for Hadassah. Conspicuous displays of wealth were frowned upon. My new stepmother was not like her. She seemed to devote her time solely to keeping her house pristine and freshly painted. This profound shift in values made my head spin. Of course, I was a sixteen-year-old girl with all the angst that went with my age. But it was hard not to feel as if the universe were doubling down on the grief it was sending my way.

Still, I managed to do what I always did: I searched for the bright side. I found two positives right away. The private school may not have had a band, but it had a dress code, and wearing a uniform every day was mandatory. I loved that idea. I didn't care if the uniform was an ugly green tunic. There would be no more agony every morning over what to wear. Another bonus? I would be driving myself to my new school.

I wasted no time in turning my rusty red Chevrolet compact into a getaway car. During my spare period every morning, I used it to escape to my aunt Lil's house. Luckily for me, Herb's older sister lived less than a ten-minute drive away. I didn't tell anyone about my visits and neither did she. We drank coffee and smoked cigarettes together, sitting in her kitchen. We laughed over how ridiculous the school uniform looked on me, especially the tie. And she would talk to me about my mother.

My aunt Lil managed to make me forget I had made no new friends and felt disconnected from my childhood ones. She reminded me that once I had had a mother named Bess, even if saying her name out loud was actively discouraged in my new stepmother's house. Aunt Lil's home, her very presence, made me feel safe and loved, there in my secret bolt-hole.

• • •

My father, his sister, and their two older brothers came from the small town of Wakaw, Saskatchewan. My grandfather ran the general store there, as did so many Jewish immigrants in prairie towns across Western Canada in the twenties and thirties. Wakaw was also famous for a footnote in Canadian history: our thirteenth prime minister, John Diefenbaker, began a criminal law practice in the town. He was friendly with my grandparents.

Like many family histories, mine is a sprawling, colourful narrative of interconnections. Even after they married and lived in Toronto as adults, the Pascoe siblings remained close. My western and eastern Canadian families converged in Toronto back in the 1940s. My father was studying dentistry at the University of Toronto when he met my mother's older brother, Sol, another dental student. They became close friends. In this friendship between two newly minted dentists about to serve in the army, one from Saskatchewan and the other from Nova Scotia, lay the origins of my tribe.

When Bessie died, our extended tribe rallied around us. But my father depended most on his beloved sister for her kindness and support, especially when it came to me. On the day of my mother's funeral, it was Aunt Lil who helped me navigate the grief-stricken mourners at our synagogue. She silently shielded me from the commotion when my Cape Breton grandmother fussed at not being able to see her daughter in the closed coffin. At the graveside, she never let go of my hand. (From their own mother, Becky, my father received cruelty rather than comfort. She didn't come to the funeral or the *shiva* and actually scolded him for thinking his grief was special. "Do you think you're the only man to ever lose his wife?" she asked him, words he never forgot.)

After I returned to school from mourning and broke my foot, Aunt Lil taught me how to knit to distract me. I certainly learned from an expert. She was famous in our family for her ability to smoke and knit at the same time. A quiet, discreet woman, Lil preferred to leave the opinions to her husband. Their home was a 1960s salon of Jewish intellectuals, so there were lots of opinions in the air. A steady stream of visitors from Israel passionately discussed Middle East politics with my uncle Harry, an ardent Zionist of that era. Aunt Lil would sit in a corner perch on the couch in their living room, her knitting needles seemingly on autopilot, or wander around the room serving coffee and pastries. I liked that she never forgot to refill the endless bowls of Smarties, our favourite chocolate candy.

Aunt Lil gave me a master class on how to be a caring aunt. My father may have been my role model for resilience, but it was his sister who showed me what empathy and compassion look like.

She listened to me, let me cry when I needed to, and made me feel that one person was truly in my corner. After I left for college, returning only during holidays, the phone always rang on my first morning back. It would be Aunt Lil, welcoming me home and asking when I would be stopping by to visit. I was usually there within twenty minutes.

• • •

That long-ago lecture at the American School of London took place on a stopover on my way back to Vancouver. I was returning home after a week of travelling in Israel with my cousin Anita, who lived there. Anita was Aunt Lil's daughter. It was my first visit to the Holy Land to see her, one that was long overdue.

Anita was ten years older, so I had never really known her while growing up. She left home in the early 1960s, eventually marrying an Israeli, having children, and making her life in Israel. Sitting in her parents' living room in Toronto, I heard all her stories from their end of the phone line. I watched her parents prepare for their annual visits to Israel, where they owned a second home in Caesarea. Aunt Lil would pack lots of children's clothes and other consumer items that were not yet available in Israel. She was always excited to show me what she was taking, especially the outfits for her two grandchildren.

Anita and I often laughed about how we appeared together in family home movies. Most of them were taken by her father, a talented amateur photographer. At family functions, I'd be in a high chair, with Anita looking like the babysitter. As adults, we shared something else to laugh about: we were both constantly being mistaken for Barbra Streisand.

It was e-mail that changed everything for us. We began corresponding in the late nineties, first as a way of practising our new digital skills, later to exchange stories about each other or our parents. Anita quickly became my electronic confidante. I could tell her anything, and I did. You're never too old to need a cousin. Fortunately for me, I had an entire village of them raising me. And aunties too.

I didn't manage to visit Israel until I was in my fifties. One reason for that was plain stubbornness. I hate when someone tells me I "should" do something, and there had been a lot of pressure to make the trip, especially when I attended a Zionist summer camp. In the mid-aughts, though, there was reason to expedite a visit: Anita was not in the greatest of health.

From the moment I arrived, we hit the ground running, visiting all the important historical sites and then some: we took in a Palestinian pop star's concert in the ancient Roman amphitheatre of Caesarea; took a day trip to Tiberius for lunch at the Sea of Galilee; sampled organic wine and cheeses in Druze country in the north. We ate a lot, smoked a lot, and laughed a lot. By that time in my career as the Expat Expert, I could throw a dart at a map and find a speaking engagement on the topic of my global living books, so I easily lined up two gigs in Jerusalem.

Israel may loom large in the world's imagination, but it's not a large country geographically speaking. That made it easy for Anita to drive us from her home in Pardes Hanna-Karkur to Jerusalem for my lectures. For two cousins discovering and delighting in each other later in life, it was an epic road trip. We belted out Broadway show tunes and left no rest stop unvisited. I learned the Hebrew phrase for "excuse me" since Anita shouted it out often, trying to get directions from pedestrians and other drivers along the way. My cousin was in the audience for both of my speaking engagements, of course, offering much-appreciated moral support. She had become my biggest cheerleader in all aspects of my life.

• • •

Despite her health challenges, Anita lived for another fifteen years after my first visit to Israel. Her many ailments finally caught up with her during the COVID-19 pandemic, when travel restrictions made it impossible for me to say goodbye in person or to get to her funeral. Luckily, I had been back to see her several more times before then.

Aunt Lil, sadly, never made it to sixty. I was still in my early twenties, working in Winnipeg, when she died from heart problems. I didn't get a chance to say goodbye to her in person either. I'm sorry she never saw me become a wife and mother myself. My close relationship with her namesake, my daughter, Lilly, remains a daily reminder of her loving care for me.

Chilling Out in Chile

IT WAS LATE 2008. The stock market had just crashed. Emotionally I was a mess, crying for no apparent reason. I was sick of expats and long removed from that life, but still constantly on the go as the Expat Expert. Now, my post-menopausal body was sending me a message. It was time to put on the brakes or face serious work burnout.

As it happened, rescue was on the horizon. I had visited Chile the previous year to lecture to the expat community in Santiago. A dynamic Chilean woman named Chica had been instrumental in organizing my lectures. We stayed in touch, and once she heard about my predicament, she invited me to come back.

"Every writer needs quiet time," she told me. "Why not find solitude in Pucon?"

Her family owned a vacation property in the popular tourist town 800 kilometres south of Santiago. Pucon is also home to an active volcano. How fun it will be, I thought, enjoying a girlfriend's company, drinking pisco sours, chilling out in Chile. Except it seemed her idea was for me to go to Pucon *alone* for an entire week at the beginning of my visit. To relax. As if.

And not only that: first I had to get there. Looking at a map of Chile, I estimated Santiago to Pucon would be a one-and-a-half-hour flight tops, probably involving some kind of small plane. My fear of flying could be controlled for such a short hop. I might even try to do it cold sober, not to miss out on the views, which I figured would be breathtaking.

"You don't actually fly to Pucon," Chica explained on the phone as we were planning my visit. "You take an overnight bus. It's a ten-and-a-half-hour ride."

I let the information sink in. "You *do* remember that I don't speak any Spanish, right?" We had discussed this language failing of mine before. Yes, she said, but that would not be an obstacle. "You don't need to speak to anyone, Robin. Besides, you'll sleep on the bus. You'll love it! They even serve a meal if you want. And our caretaker, Carlos, will meet you at the bus station in Pucon." My heart slowed slightly, until she added, "By the way, Carlos doesn't speak English."

· · ·

Chica saw me off at the bus station in Santiago. She fretted over me like a mother sending her child off to summer camp, even boarding the bus to chat up my fellow passengers. In my bag were some flash cards my Spanish-speaking daughter had made me. There were many useful phrases translated and ready for me. Unfortunately, they didn't include *My seat belt is broken!* That one would have come in handy right after the bus pulled out of the station.

The bus was a double-decker, and my ticket was for the upper level, in business class: a large seat that reclined fully, a pillow and blanket handed out after our meal, and a television monitor. With no seat belt to hold me in, however, I felt unsteady on the dark, winding roads. I actually fell out of my seat in the middle of the night as we navigated a particularly sharp bend in the road.

As a long-time cellphone resister, I didn't own one. Chica had lent me an old phone that had once belonged to her youngest son. Conveniently, the number for "Mom" was on speed dial. I lay awake the entire night, the phone clutched in a near death grip, causing pins and needles to run up my arms. Fortunately, I didn't accidentally disconnect it. I wasn't sure how to turn it back on.

"Don't think of this as a test," Rodney, my reassuring husband, had said when I called him before leaving, nervous about spending the week alone, unable to speak to anyone and in close proximity to an active volcano. "If you want to return to Santiago after a few days, no one will think any less of you."

Except, of course, for me.

•   •   •

My comfort zone was eleven thousand kilometres and a hemisphere away when I stepped through the door of an expensively decorated, eight-bedroom recreational home, a scene ripped from the glossy pages of a home design magazine. The styling was camera-ready. Even the whimsical tchotchkes matched the decor. As someone known to run screaming out of IKEA, overwhelmed by the challenges of colour coordination and too much choice, I found the home both beautiful and demoralizing.

The fireplace in the living room could have graced the lobby of a five-star hotel. There appeared to be a wood stove in every bedroom. Oversized couches to get comfortable in were everywhere, upholstered in soothing colours, with matching cushions and cozy throw blankets. A set of sliding glass doors opened onto a terrace with an unobstructed million-dollar view, at least when the clouds cleared, of the famous volcano, snow-topped and glorious.

I was left alone to my own devices, quite literally, in a mansion out of *Lifestyles of the Rich and Famous* at the bottom of the world. There was almost nothing to distract me, and this discombobulated me terribly. There was no WiFi and social media barely existed. Netflix was not yet dreamed of, and neither Skype nor Zoom had been invented.

To soothe my OCD soul, I quickly devised a routine, beginning at 6:30 a.m. with coffee and journaling, and ending with lights out at 11:00 p.m. In between, I soon found things to occupy me. For e-mail and a caffe latte, I wandered into town in the mornings to an internet café on the main street, a fifteen-minute walk I could easily navigate with directions drawn on a scrap of paper in those days before Google Maps. Next, a stop at the grocery store to buy supplies for the fresh salads I lived on, heaped with avocados that were plentiful, fresh breads baked on the spot, and my daily ration of half bottles of Chilean white wine. The labels didn't matter as long as I had one bottle for lunch and another one for dinner. I would temper the wine with long, refreshing afternoon naps. A carton of Kool Light duty-free cigarettes along with a few books and magazines, a portable DVD player borrowed from Chica, a stack of DVD movies and, strangely, the first three seasons of *Two and a Half Men*, which I had never watched, completed my stash of diversions. Charlie Sheen turned out be good raunchy company.

To be fair, I wasn't completely alone. Carlos, the caretaker, slipped in and out of the house every day to build and maintain the fires, beginning at around 7:00 a.m. Chile was heading into summer, but in Pucon, being so far south in the country, the weather was brisk.

I tried to write, sitting at a table set up outside on the terrace, where I could smoke. I did manage to compose one personal essay, "The Week I Stopped Speaking," which would later be rejected like most others I attempted to have published in Canada's "national" newspaper, the *Globe and Mail*. Once, the *Globe* had accepted a piece of mine, an emotional essay about my late mother. It memorably ran on Referendum Day in 1995, when the whole country needed a good cry.

In trying to escape the noise of my regular life, I had ended up in a place that was anything but quiet. The wind didn't just howl. It shrieked. There was no weather pattern to explain why, Chica said, when I queried her after testing out the speed dial on her son's old cellphone. When her three sons were young, she told me, she would hustle them out into the garden, arms high in the air, to let the intense wind wash over them. I attempted that one windy afternoon, only to spot Carlos standing at the living-room window watching me. Oops.

And the dogs! The barking never seemed to stop. It got louder and closer once the local pack figured out I had empanadas in my knapsack. I had bought a fragrant supply of the meat pastries one day to have for dinner. The aroma was so deliciously powerful that half a dozen mangy, very hungry dogs followed me home. As I increased my speed, they began to chase me. Breathlessly, I slammed the gate to the property shut on their twitchy noses. That night, I dreamed my body was discovered on the road, dead and tattered.

Still, in the end, I passed the-week-that-was-not-a-test with flying colours. I barely remember the bus ride back to Santiago. That's because I slept almost the whole way, strapped safely into my seat, the borrowed phone no longer the focus of my anxiety. Truth be told, I felt pretty damn good about myself.

•   •   •

I met the famous Chilean psychic Eduardo Godoy when Chica hosted a dinner party at her home in my honour. Eduardo, a good friend of hers, and his partner, a local doctor, attended along with other local luminaries, including the American ambassador to Chile and his Colombian wife, who worked for the World Bank.

The guest list was well above my pay grade. When I tried explaining that to my lovely hostess, she was perplexed to learn I suffer from terrible social anxiety. She had seen me lecture confidently in front of hundreds of people. But work was one thing. I had to sell books, after all. Social situations unnerve me, especially when they involve diplomats. With people I have never met before, my social phobia returns like muscle memory, a throwback to our days in the foreign service when Rodney's position was so lowly, we attended the odd function where literally no one spoke to us. (Of course, once that was because we were at the wrong cocktail party in a large Bangkok hotel. It took us almost half an hour to realize it, since we were so used to people walking right past us.) I fretted incessantly over what I was wearing on those occasions, never fancy or fashionable enough, and don't get me started on how bad my hair looked on postings to countries with hairdressers perplexed by naturally curly hair. With age, my phobia about parties and events with dressed-up people had only worsened.

Nonetheless, there I was at an elegant dinner party in Chica's torch-lit garden, with conversations in Spanish swirling around me and everyone looking like they had just stepped out of an American Express ad. The obvious solution was pisco sours. I definitely planned to live up to the jolly invitation sent out for the party: *One pisco, two pisco, three pisco, floor.*

As it happened, I was seated at dinner with Eduardo and his partner. He spoke no English and was almost deaf as well, so his partner and Chica served as my interpreters over the course of the evening. Eduardo told me at one point that the American ambassador had a dark aura around his head and definitely wasn't feeling well. I didn't see any aura, dark or otherwise, but sure enough, the ambassador and his wife rose from the table minutes later to take an early leave. Allergies, they said. I drank another pisco sour.

Scoring a professional session with Eduardo was no easy matter for ordinary mortals. Due to high demand, he opened his phone line for appointments for only one hour on the first Monday of every month, between 10:00 and 11:00 a.m. Luckily, though, I had connections. A few days after the dinner party, I met Eduardo at his apartment. An appearance in a Discovery Channel documentary had given him some notoriety. Urban legend or not, the story was that when a James Bond movie crew had been in Chile to shoot some scenes earlier that year, Daniel Craig had insisted on meeting Eduardo. That made me barely two degrees of separation from James Bond!

I had done my homework and brought with me a list of seven questions about my future and a photo of my family in which everyone's eyes could be seen clearly. That was the only prep necessary, besides suspending disbelief about a parallel world of people watching over me during the hour and a half I spent with him. I took copious notes that are hard to read now and I smoked furiously.

Do I really want to share what transpired in my session, with Chica there as simultaneous translator? No.

"There is nothing more boring than hearing about someone else's therapy." Those exact words appeared on a feedback form after a presentation I delivered at a large American conference on mobility. The subject had been my latest book, *A Moveable Marriage*. Expat marriage as a topic was always a tough sell. This particular meeting was held barely two weeks after 9/11, and the conference was poorly attended. (Another attendee had written, "I was too distracted by the speaker's wild hair and giant glasses to hear a word she said," proving that someone in the United States still had a sense of humour.)

While Eduardo predicted a few things that could later be seen as happening in our daughter's life, he didn't come close to nailing what lay ahead for me. I wonder if Daniel Craig had better luck. Maybe he found out before anyone else who would eventually replace him as James Bond.

• • •

On my final night in Santiago, I went out to dinner with some acquaintances I had met on my previous visit. I entertained them with stories about my week alone in Pucon, including the fact that the volcano had decided to start smoking on my last day there. Which led me to pronounce: "And speaking of smoking, all I really needed while I was there was a puff of some good Chilean *ganja*. I enjoyed the Chilean white wines, but a toke would have made it just perfect."

Being from Vancouver, a city *High Times* magazine once declared to be not only the home of the best weed in the world but also the best place to smoke it, I often throw the subject of marijuana into my conversations. I am an unabashedly proud pothead (who knows better than to *ever* smoke pot or boast about it in, say, Singapore or Malaysia, where the authorities execute offenders). I had sampled local products on several of my solo journeys. Not for nothing had I lectured multiple times in Holland, where the local coffee houses made it easy to indulge.

"Do you really want to try some South American pot?" asked one of my dinner companions. "I can arrange that." Of course he could. He was at least twenty-five years younger and was obviously amused at the idea of helping a middle-aged woman score some weed in Santiago. We set off in his sports car while he worked his contacts from his car phone. It was quite late when we pulled up in front of a large apartment building. He turned off the motor.

"I'm just going to run up and get it for you," he told me. "The key is in the ignition, so you can move the car if someone comes by." *Wait, what?* Where the hell would I move the car *to* at midnight in Santiago? We didn't appear to be in a bad neighbourhood. In fact, it looked like a respectable part of town. After ten minutes, my companion emerged from the building and gave me a thumbs-up. As he got behind the wheel, he tossed me a small Tupperware container.

"He even threw in some papers for you. Can you roll?"

"Of course!"

"Mom" was waiting up for me when I got home. I showed her the package.

"Do you think we have to return the Tupperware when it's empty?" Chica asked.

"I wouldn't have a clue who to give it back to," I said. "I'll leave it with you when I leave Santiago."

A good plan, we agreed. In the meantime, we came up with an even better one for the contents of the container.

• THREE •

Interregnum

AS I CREPT towards the age of sixty, I was filled with angst. I had decided to stop writing books for my global tribe, but what should I do instead? I had weathered challenging transitions before, but the very idea of retirement put me into a bewildering betwixt-and-between state. On some days, I couldn't imagine leaving the working world. On others, I questioned my resistance. It was sensible to consider slowing down. I'd been lecturing and travelling non-stop for years, after all. But the concept of facing a day without purpose, my identity twisting in the wind, frankly terrified me.

No such ambivalence showed up in my dreams. They turned into nightmares. In one frequent vision, I was trapped in an airport departure lounge waiting for a flight that had been delayed. When I glanced up at the board to check its status, the flight number wasn't there. It didn't even exist. Transparent enough? Other nights, I'd be on frantic, futile searches for my hotel room or my gate for a flight. I'd awaken exhausted, my heart pounding, as if I had really been running. And sweating too, long after I'd finished with menopause. I could rarely fall back to sleep after those nocturnal panic attacks. Instead, I would lie awake, trying to figure out before the sun rose just what the hell I should do with the rest of my life.

I had few role models to inspire me. My mother had been only forty-four when she died. My father was so determined to keep on working as a dentist (to avoid being at home all day with his second wife) that he rehabilitated himself after a heart attack in his late seventies. He ended up practising dentistry for more than fifty-five years, before dropping dead of a massive coronary between patients one day, two weeks short of his eightieth birthday. His dental assistant found him keeled over in his private office, clutching a patient's X-rays in his hand. He'd been golfing only a few days earlier. My father-in-law, likewise, was still working when he died, way too early, at sixty-four. A pediatrician with an active practice, he also suffered a fatal coronary. His timing couldn't have been worse—not that he had any choice about it. He died two days before the birth in Ottawa of his grandson, our son Jay, whom we named after him. My brother Laurie held my hand during my scheduled Caesarian section so that Rodney could be in Winnipeg to comfort his mother.

As I contemplated retirement, I began reading whatever I could lay my hands on that addressed my issues. It would be in the title poem of the 2012 collection *Writers Writing Dying*, by the Pulitzer Prize–winning poet C. K. Williams, that I found my feelings perfectly captured. "Think, write, write, think; just keep galloping faster and you won't even notice you're dead."

• • •

My days as the Expat Expert had ended with neither panic nor drama. The decision to retire from that role came to me naturally, on a speaking tour in Southeast Asia in the spring of 2009. During my lectures on that trip, I worried I might start hearing negative comments from the audience: "Is she *still* doing this?" or "When did *she* last live as an expat, anyway?" Solo travel, a blur of cheap hotels, lunatic travel itineraries, and couch-surfing to save money had all lost their charm by then. Moreover, my bad habits on the road disgusted me. Chain-smoking and drinking too much vodka to cope with flying were not sustainable behaviours. It was time for me to step back, preferably while people were still keen to hear me. The right moment presented itself in Bangkok, on the final day of my three-week tour.

I'd been invited to speak to the new mothers of the Bangkok Association of Mothers and Babies International (BAMBI), the support group for which I'd first volunteered as a newsletter writer twenty-five years earlier. The venue for the event was an auditorium in Samitivej Hospital, where our daughter Lilly had been born. Dr. Tanit, the Thai obstetrician who had delivered her, was there, seated beside his wife Mel, the midwife who had founded the group. Also lending me moral support that day were my Thai girlfriend Amporn and her husband Pum. Amporn had done a journalism degree at Carleton a year after me. Rodney and I were among a handful of *farangs* honoured to be invited to her Bangkok wedding. Over a flavourful lunch after my lecture to the new moms, I learned from Amporn that our old apartment building on Sukhumvit Soi 16 was still standing in its lane, even amidst the urban development of recent decades. My hotel was in the same neighbourhood, so that afternoon, I decided to head out and take a closer look.

Starbucks outlets and Lexus dealerships had replaced the noodle stands, VD clinics, and massage parlours with names like Man's House that had lined the Sukhumvit Road of my era.

As I turned down Soi 16, my memories shimmered like the apparitions that had once appeared in the early morning mist: Buddhist monks in saffron-coloured robes walking in pairs with their begging bowls, a goat or two trailing behind them. My mind flashed back to the rainy seasons, when the lane would always flood. To reach our building, we had to walk through filthy sewage water, often rising as high as our knees. A plastic bag or two might drift by as we waded, or a dog paddling frantically to keep afloat. Urban legend had it that Thai street dogs had been murderers in previous lives. And how could I forget the occasional sight of an elephant hauling garbage past the entrance to our laneway? The tantalizing aroma from a food cart selling *guay tiew gai*, my favourite chicken noodle soup, seemed real enough that day.

I gazed up at our old balcony. Once, it had held the birds we bought for Lilly at Bangkok's popular weekend market, two budgies we named after Thai generals. Later, we brought home Big Guy, a large, noisy, colourful parrot who lived in a wooden cage crafted to resemble a Thai spirit house, until he managed to eat his own perch and flew away.

As I walked back to the hotel to prepare for my lecture that evening, I decided it would be my last one. I'd had a good run as the Expat Expert, but I felt my work was done.

• • •

When an invitation to speak in Moscow arrived in my e-mail a few months later, my resolve to put expats behind me wavered. *Maybe just one last time*, I told myself. I'd never been to Russia. But when I ran into some roadblocks with my hosts, I abandoned my travel plans. I didn't want that kind of stress anymore. (My decision turned out to be fortuitous. On March 29, 2010, a day when I would have been visiting, twin terrorist bombings in the Moscow subway killed forty people and injured even more, throwing the city into a crisis.)

So I was back to grappling with retirement. And it seemed my own ego was getting in the way. I'd never thought much about my ego, other than to assure myself from time to time that I brilliantly kept it in check. I was keeping it real, I thought, feet firmly planted on the ground, never making a fuss about myself, staying low-key and self-deprecating. Now I could see just how fragile my ego was. I wasn't a household name, though there were certainly those who recognized me from my work. My previous successes counted for nothing in my own mind. And I seemed intent on discounting everything that was going well in my life: some terrific non-working adventures with friends and family; building houses on an excursion to Cambodia; theatre weekends in New York City with Lilly, who by then was pursuing her Ph.D. at Cornell, in upstate New York. I tagged along on some of Rodney's more interesting business trips too. We visited souks in Marrakesh, rode elephants in Jaipur, listened to chamber music in Prague, stayed in French colonial hotels in Vietnam, and browsed the Grand Bazaar of Istanbul. But I couldn't stop myself from creating a blog called *The Desperate Traveler* so I would have something to do while Rodney worked, and my professional envy grew. I was behaving like a spoiled, ungrateful brat.

Writers who became internet stars made me furiously jealous. How the hell did they manage to go viral? I wanted to find out, so I came up with three other writing projects after stepping back from the Expat Expert. First, there was *The Year I Took Piano Lessons*, a blog inspired by *Julie & Julia*, the 2009 movie in which Meryl Streep plays gourmet chef Julia Child. Amy Adams starred as the real-life Julie Powell, an aspiring blogger who decides to cook one of Child's famous French cuisine recipes every day for a year and to post a blog about it. I was keen to study piano again before my fingers were too arthritic. Why not take lessons and blog about the experience of resurrecting the pianist in me forty years after quitting as a teenager?

I managed quite well, studying with my daughter's old piano teacher, but when she suggested one day that for fun I play in a recital, I was thankful to be an adult. I firmly declined. Memories from my youth were etched into my brain. My father had certainly never let me forget the time I showed up for a recital at the Royal Conservatory of Toronto wearing beat-up old black running shoes with holes in them. I blogged about those early experiences and offered what I thought were amusing stories about returning to the piano decades later. But by the end of a year, only a handful of people had read my entries. I was probably related to most of them. Still, I told myself, nothing was really lost. I could sit down at the piano and play it again.

Next, I followed a piece of advice from a career counsellor and switched over from the print medium to video. Maybe that would jump-start my creativity. Since I had spent my early professional years in broadcasting, I knew how to speak to a camera. Here was a chance to feed two birds with the same seed. I created a YouTube channel and posted an 18-part series of video lectures. Ten years later, a pandemic would force the entire world online.

Back then, though, my five-minute videos gained little traction. I felt bitter every time I noted which other YouTube videos (especially those about expat life) were receiving thousands of views, while my own offerings languished with a barely single-digit viewership. Not for the first time in my writing life, I questioned whether I had vastly overrated myself. On the plus side, I began a creative collaboration with the talented Vancouver videographer Jennifer Lee, which continues to this day.

In my third and final attempt to find my online groove, I channelled my anxiety into a fictional blog called *The Rest of My Life.* I composed fifty-five 500-word installments supposedly written by a character named Joelly Schuster, a diplomatic wife who had repatriated to Canada from China after being ditched by her philandering husband. My idea of a novella in blog form (I called it a *blogella*, in the hopes of starting a new craze) also failed to generate any steam. Some of the people who read it even thought Joelly was me. Oh dear. That couldn't be good. I was running out of ideas.

Finally, I considered tackling another full-length book. I had proposed several book projects to publishers over the years. All of them focused on the impact of technology and social media on society and our interactions with one another. I was fifteen years too early for a book I pitched about the distressing rise of narcissism and the waning of empathy thanks to the internet and Facebook. There were no takers for that one, not even with the catchy title I hated to waste—*Me, Myself, but Mostly I.*

Rodney had a front-row seat to my frustration. He had started working from home a few years earlier. Our son, Jay, was also in the house every day, working alongside his father in a new business venture. It was difficult for both of them to listen to me slamming doors and screaming at my computer. Despite the dead ends I hit, though, I was committed to continuing. I would find some way to work until the bitter end, just as my father had done. I would simply have to redefine what a writing life looked like to me. The business of communications is a big tent, I reminded myself, with room for books, blogs, and many other forms of content. Working with words, in some fashion, would be my way forward.

I didn't know it yet, but Rodney had a rescue plan in mind for me, one that fit perfectly with my writing goals. Before long, he would ask me to put my communications skills and global experience to work creating a brand for the company we had bet our family farm on. At an age when conventional wisdom deemed we should be put out to pasture, Rodney and I risked our North Vancouver house on a bear. A Maple Bear. Neither one of us could have predicted the decade that followed.

The Carry-On Imperative

I'M THAT SMUG carry-on traveller everyone knows. The one who self-righteously boasts about her minimalist luggage choices, as if the smaller the bag, the greater the virtue. Nothing could be further from the truth. My tiny roller bag only signals that *I own very few clothes*. Not a single dress, skirt, jacket, tunic, or fancy outfit of any description hangs in my closet. Not one. I threw most of my clothes into green garbage bags over fifteen years ago, tossed them all into my car, and headed for my local Salvation Army Thrift Store. I gave away my full-length mirror while I was at it. The clothing I was donating had not been worn in years and was collecting dust. Better someone else should get some use out of my glad rags.

My clothes anxieties, as you have read, date back to when I was twelve. After my mother died, my wardrobe began triggering anxiety attacks far beyond the run-of-the-mill, I-have-nothing-to-wear complaints of my girlfriends. To my mind, the sorry state of my wardrobe screamed: *Who the hell is dressing her? Oh right, no one. Poor Robin.*

I don't recall having an aversion to dressing up before my mother died. True, Bessie was a casual dresser. She lived in her golf clothes and would probably have embraced activewear if it had been around at the time. She took me to buy new shoes before the start of every school year. But my memory bank is empty of any excursions to buy new clothes. That might be because I wore a lot of hand-me-downs from my older cousin Joey, who herself had to wear castoffs from her older sister Lynda. My cousins attended a different school, so my fellow students could not easily figure out the source of the *J* embroidered over my heart or the sweater with an *L* on it I wore once.

It wasn't just hand-me-downs with the wrong initials on them, though, that made me look as if I'd raided the bargain basement at Eaton's, the iconic Canadian department store. There was also the matter of *the dress*. Dresses confounded me, and the simple shift I tried to make in my home economics class a few months after my mother died haunts me still. Miss Tuz, our teacher, provided us with patterns to work from. They might as well have been war maps of troop movements, for how impossible I found them to follow. Still, after managing to find some powder-blue cotton fabric at Eaton's, I was hopeful I could manage my assignment without asking for anyone's help. Who would I have asked, anyway? My two older brothers? They were great with my math homework but couldn't possibly weigh in on domestic arts. And my aunt Lil was a knitter and not into sewing. In the end, it didn't matter. I was undone by the darts. I still don't see the reason for darts. They're diabolical to sew properly, and my shift turned out to be a disaster. Unfortunately, Miss Tuz deemed it wearable.

There was to be a fashion show at school when our dresses were completed, and all parents would be invited to attend. That meant the moms, of course, because the event would be held during the day, when dads were working. As I imagined my recently widowed father cancelling his dental patients to spend an afternoon in a room full of sympathetic mothers, I began to fret immediately.

On the day of the fashion show, I begged my father to let me stay home. I faked a temperature. I pretended to vomit. I pulled the bedcovers over my head and insisted I was coming down with something serious. But Herb had cleared his afternoon for the fashion show, and to be honest, he had his own agenda. He wanted to demonstrate that everything was just fine in our bereaved household. Look how wonderfully we were all coping with this huge hole in our lives! My shift was too tight (I blamed the darts), and I walked down the makeshift runway looking like the creaky Tin Man in *The Wizard of Oz*. It would have been easier to walk in front of my entire school buck naked.

Afterwards, as Herb mingled with the moms over refreshments, it wasn't my dress that was on their minds. It was the good-looking widower in his mid-forties. *A dentist too, did you hear?* I tossed my shift into the garbage the minute I got home, setting a lifelong pattern for dealing with sartorial anxiety.

As an adult, I adopted a less fraught approach to dressing. I narrowed my choices to blue jeans, black jeans, white T-shirts, black T-shirts, white blouses, and black blouses. Okay, with maybe the occasional dash of colour. I love anything turquoise. Never anything powder blue. I don't need built-in closets for my designer shoes, funky hats, or purses, since I have never collected any. My accessories are limited to costume jewellery acquired in faraway places, mostly at airport gift shops, or purchased online from the American retailer Chico's. I avoid belts too, and definitely no scarves. I hate scarves. They feed directly into my fashion inferiority complex, since I'm not a chic French woman. They are the only people who can really wear scarves well, in my opinion. All of this explains why I could store my entire wardrobe in a carry-on case if I had to, or most of it anyway.

• • •

Rodney and I had been married for nearly thirty years when he first suggested I work alongside him for Maple Bear Global Schools, our international bilingual education brand. Despite the conventional wisdom, working together turned out to be one of the best things to ever happen to us. There's nothing like a shared purpose to strengthen a relationship—not to mention an excuse to visit just about anywhere in the world and call it a business trip. Still, Rodney has his ways and I have mine. If the twain were ever to meet, as the saying goes, we needed some ground rules to keep us on course while we travelled non-stop building our company. We came up with five top travel commandments.

#1 Thou shalt not wait for luggage.

The carry-on imperative was our prime directive. It was compulsory, whether we would be on the road for a week or travelling for a month through multiple continents and climates. Luckily for me, a woman can carry a very large purse. Mind you, this aging woman needed a second one just to accommodate all the pills I haul around. Otherwise, packing was simple. Limiting my sartorial choices was already my wont. And who would be looking at *me*, anyway? I ensured I was never in the pictures by taking all of them myself.

Travelling with only a carry-on bag does come with a few stresses that have nothing to do with packing the right outfits. Getting even the smallest case on board can sometimes be tricky. Some airlines and airports impose weight restrictions that are even more minimalistic than the size of the bags themselves. Vienna's airport springs to mind. Austrians are allowed just 8 kilos, less than half the weight restriction for carry-on luggage in North America. Eight kilos is about one T-shirt and a few pairs of panties, by my estimation, and maybe a pair of pants, after you account for the weight of the bag itself. Aside from facing weight restrictions, I've also witnessed fights over the limited space in overhead bins that crossed into *Hunger Games* territory. Worst of all, though, was when our bags were taken away to be checked at the last minute before boarding. Maple Bear's president and CEO never handled that consequence of our carry-on commandment very well.

#2 Thou shalt not accept an upgrade if your travelling companion is not offered one.

Rodney and I were flying to Prague when the need for this commandment became apparent. We would be celebrating a milestone wedding anniversary there as well as doing business. Just before we boarded our first flight, from Vancouver, Rodney, as a super elite traveller with Air Canada, was offered an upgrade to business class. I was not. When he accepted it, I was livid. *You're joking, right?* I wondered aloud how many times the gate agent had seen this scene play out, because it was clear she was enjoying our exchange.

"We're off to celebrate our thirtieth wedding anniversary," I said to her. *Hint hint.*

"How nice!" she said before turning to Rodney. "Sir, you can board now. Ma'am, you can wait over there."

I didn't make a scene. I just made sure my husband's life was a living hell after we landed. Thanks to our rule, he never again accepted an upgrade without me.

#3 Thou shalt not get shit-faced drunk on a plane.

Rodney had waited a long time for this commandment. His years of embarrassment at flying with a noticeably inebriated wife had finally come to an end, if not for my liver then for the sake of our marriage. He was done braving dirty looks from other passengers because of me. There would be no more having to toss out the barf bags when I overdid it and an end to the mutterings of disgusted fellow passengers. "Finally, she's passed out!"

Happily, a miracle occurred. I woke up one day soon after I started working for Maple Bear to discover I was no longer afraid of flying. It might have been my advancing age, or maybe it was the fact that too many people close to me were dying or already dead from illness. Going down suddenly in a fiery plane crash seemed infinitely preferable to a protracted death from cancer, hooked up to tubes. Whatever the reason, my fear of flying literally up and left me and it has never returned. For our relationship, it was a plus. My liver also celebrated.

#4 Thou shalt hand over all dirty clothes to the hotel laundry, no matter the cost.

Surveying our room one day at the Sheraton Hotel in Tel Aviv, I thought I had mistakenly entered the hotel's laundry room. The president and CEO's underwear, socks, and shirts covered every surface not taken up by my bras, panties, and T-shirts. As I had done on several earlier trips, I'd spent the first hour after our check-in the previous evening hand-washing the contents of both our carry-on bags. We were in Israel on a short stopover to see my cousin Anita, after business meetings in Dubai. There were no direct air links between the UAE and Israel at the time, so Rodney, an ardent birder, had decided that the most direct route to Tel Aviv from Dubai was through Addis Ababa. *Huh?* He confessed to "always having a hankering to see the endemic bird species of the Ethiopian Highlands." Right. Who doesn't? Well, I don't, for starters, but I wanted to see my cousin, and the only way, apparently, was to tour Ethiopia for six days first (a story for another day). The point is, by the time we got to Israel, our bags were full of dirty clothes, and the director of global communications was apparently expected to attend to them. With that commandment, not anymore.

#5 Thou shalt wait at least 24 hours after landing before trying to canoodle the director of global communications.

When Rodney used to travel non-stop without me, in the earlier days of our marriage, I often wondered (out loud, which he never appreciated) if the road warrior only returned home for clean shirts and sex. In my talks for expat audiences, I introduced the concept of the 24-hour holding rule after a business trip: *everyone to their respective corners for one day.* That always guaranteed an easy laugh, at least from the women. The men usually gave me dirty looks, and so did Rodney the first time we arrived together in Brazil. It had taken us endless hours of flying, waiting in lines, and riding in taxis before we could finally check in to our hotel. All I wanted was a shower and a good night's sleep. The president and CEO had other ideas, which is how the fifth travel commandment was established.

The simplicity of travelling carry-on fits nicely with my goal of getting lighter later in life. Making sure someone got some use out of my closet full of clothes also brought me a lot of joy. Maybe Marie Kondo has it right after all.

Wide Awake in the World

IN THE QUIRKY 2006 film *Stranger Than Fiction*, comedian Will Ferrell plays a man forced to listen to a woman narrating his life as it happens, in a voice only he can hear. Emma Thompson plays the fiction writer whose words are literally stuck in his head. In one hilarious scene, Ferrell walks down an empty street shouting at the invisible person torturing him. "Shut up! Shut up! Shut up!" he screams.

It could be the battle cry of insomniacs everywhere. That relentless inner voice infuriates the sleepless soul lying awake at 2:00 a.m., at 3:36 a.m., at 4:21 and 5:35. Sleep is elusive when the mind refuses to shut the fuck up.

My insomnia started when I was a girl. Sunday nights were always sleepless, because I would fret over returning to school on Monday morning. The night before summer camp began, excitement kept me awake and raiding my new comic book stash. As I got older, there were early morning flights to worry about missing. Now, it can be a night when meditation is useless or too much screen time on my tablet has made my eyes spin. On trips outside of Canada, where cannabis is legal now, I'm deprived of the best and most reliable sleep aid on the market. On those sleepless nights, I flat out beg the universe to just club me over the head already.

Our peripatetic life hasn't helped. My sleep challenges ratcheted up to a whole new level when I was pregnant with our son, Jay. We were in between foreign service assignments at the time, living in the Gatineau Hills of Quebec. In my seventh month, I was incapable of drifting off at night *at all*. None of my home remedies worked. Not that some of them were recommended for a pregnant woman, like the three fingers of scotch I threatened to pour down my throat in the middle of the night. All right, I *did* pour three fingers of scotch down my throat one night. Sleeplessness breeds madness and desperation.

My insomnia got even more acute after Jay was born. I developed a condition known as restless leg syndrome. It can present in pregnancy, as mine apparently did. Prescribed medication for it was still a few years away. In the meantime, the foreign service posted us to China.

• • •

Lying wide wake in Beijing was no picnic. Making it even more unpleasant was the less than salubrious condition of our staff quarters. The place was depressing enough in the daytime. It looked worse—much worse—in the middle of the night.

We lived in a ground-floor apartment in a high-rise building in Jianguomenwai, a diplomatic housing compound. Back then, diplomats and journalists and their families were kept away from ordinary citizens. Our apartment building sat directly across from a building famous for taking a bullet on the day the tanks rolled down the main thoroughfare, after the Tiananmen Square massacre a year earlier. I didn't find that comforting. And we quickly learned that cleaning the apartment was pointless.

The dust that layered everything returned within hours. The shades on our government-issued lamps were thick with grit that blew in from the Gobi Desert, which filtered through the shoddily sealed windows. Don't get me started on the bathrooms.

My girlfriends and I would cruise past traditional Chinese homes known as *hutongs* while out riding our bikes. With cabbages piled high like firewood outside their doors and a haze of smoke lingering from the coal braziers used for cooking, they served as a good reminder that as bad as we thought our places were, we were enjoying privileges not yet given to most Chinese people. That would change when China's economic transformation accelerated beginning in the mid-nineties, and high-end condos and houses began to proliferate. We had the distinction of living in Beijing during a brief interregnum in China's second great leap forward. The country has since jumped from the stone age to the space age, from the Flintstones to the Jetsons.

Several garbage dumpsters sat directly in front of our entrance, breeding an army of cockroaches that invaded our kitchen and the rest of our place too. Jay reported one morning that a cockroach had run across his bed in the night. We convinced him it was a dream, but we knew the truth. Everyone was aware our homes were bugged by the Chinese security bureau, but it took us several months to realize that real bugs were also ensconced. The eggs of those creepy-crawlies hatched inside the light fixtures, including the chandelier in our dining room, where we entertained other diplomats and journalists. One cockroach would make it back to Canada, sheltered inside our piano.

In the middle of the night, unable to sleep, I would crawl to the kitchen for a glass of water. Turning on the light disturbed the cockroaches, sending the ugly creatures scurrying up and down the walls and over the appliances. This freaked me out every time. As I smoked my duty-free cigarettes and stared out the filthy windows, the security bars made me feel like we were living in a cage. Another high-rise building that faced our kitchen had a disturbing legend attached to it: an expat wife was rumoured to have leaped off its roof. Maybe, like me, she was sleepless and counting cockroaches.

One night, my restlessness was so bad it awakened Lilly. My poor seven-year-old discovered her agitated mother jumping around the living room at 4:00 a.m. Insomnia may feel like a solitary hell, but it impacts anyone nearby trying to get a good night's sleep. Just ask my long-suffering husband. Some nights, I wanted to smother Rodney with a pillow because his sleeping—as a *New Yorker* cartoon I came upon put it so brilliantly—was keeping me awake.

• • •

When a sleep disorder meets jet lag, the outcome is unbearable. After flying through multiple time zones, many a traveller will head to bed as soon as the infamous jet lag veil descends, pulling down the eyelids, making it impossible to remain awake a moment longer. An upset stomach often mutes hunger pains. At 3:00 am, eyes spring open and the traveller is raring to go. And starving.

The sleep-disordered traveller will also retire early, hopeful that exhaustion will knock her out. But she tosses and turns instead, remaining wide awake, staring at the ceiling and checking the clock. She can binge-watch half a season of *The West*

Wing or *Law & Order*, and still no sign of sleep. She pops another Advil PM, or a Tylenol PM, or an antihistamine with a sleep aid in it. Maybe it's cough medicine. Over-the-counter sleep remedies sometimes work for a while, until they don't. Or, as with the notorious U-Dream Full Night sleep remedy, work like a charm until they are pulled from the market for having prescription medication in them.

After fifteen years of taking it, my prescription medication for restless leg syndrome no longer got the job done. I tapered off it not long before I began travelling with Rodney for Maple Bear full time. Instead, I tried natural remedies like melatonin, acupuncture, meditation, and hypnosis. I gave up alcohol in case it was hurting my chances of falling asleep, not helping them. Absolutely nothing worked. (But I stopped drinking altogether for a long time—a silver lining to my torture.)

Given the hectic travel itineraries Rodney and I embarked upon while building Maple Bear, I stared at a lot of different ceilings in very faraway places. Half-delirious with frustration, I was convinced that the flashing red lights of the smoke detectors were really secret messages. Wide awake on airplanes, I listened as my fellow passengers snored, farted, and cried out in the darkened cabin. Rodney, of course, could fall asleep right away on a plane and only awakened in time for breakfast.

•   •   •

The surreality of my sleeplessness reached its apex in India. Rodney and I were on a holiday in Rajasthan, testing out a new plan to squeeze tourism into our business trips. I was happy to see a famous region of India I had always wanted to visit.

I couldn't wait to get to Udaipur in particular, since it had been a stand-in for the princely state of Mirat in Granada TV's *Jewel in the Crown*, a favourite series of mine. I wasn't disappointed. I was sleepless in Jaipur but consoled myself that riding an elephant shuttle up to the famous Amber Fort, as we did one morning, did not require a good night's sleep. Someone else would be driving the elephant.

After an unbearable night in Rajasthan, though, I came to a decision. I wanted drugs again. The prescription kind. Natural methods weren't helping, and I had run out of new over-the-counter medications to try. I just couldn't take another night of staring at the ceiling. It was once possible in India to buy almost any medication from so-called street pharmacies. When I tried to find a tranquilizing benzodiazepine, however, I discovered that the days of street drug sales were over. I would need a doctor to prescribe something for me.

The manager of Maple Bear's Delhi office kindly arranged an appointment for me at a small private clinic not far from our hotel after we returned to the capital. She insisted on accompanying me, which was very nice of her. But she also decided to include herself in my consultation. In her brightly coloured, elegant sari, beautifully made up and accessorized, she watched me, the western woman in a black Gap T-shirt pulled on over jeans, dark circles under my eyes, being weighed and looking none too happy about it. I had no idea what my weight had to do with my insomnia, but it was distressing to discover I had packed on five pounds of what would eventually become the Maple Bear twenty, and it was worse having an audience. As I was ushered into the doctor's private office, our manager came too, becoming so engaged I felt like asking if she had any thoughts on my choice of sleep medication. Eventually, *we* left with a prescription for Valium.

Does this story have a happy ending? Hell, no. I needed a mega amount of something to knock me out, but I was stuck with the prescribed baby dose. In desperation, I popped a second tablet in the middle of the night. But just as sleep was finally overtaking me, a *muezzin* issued the day's first call to prayers from a nearby mosque. The volume of the blaring loudspeakers made it seem as if they were directly under our hotel window. Which, as it happens, they were. The distinctive sound that alerts the faithful pulled me right back to consciousness, and I remained wide awake, pissed off, for the rest of the night.

Only another insomniac can understand the agitation sleeplessness whips up and the after-effects: sleep-walking the following day, raw and vulnerable, utterly convinced the world sucks. The consequences of complaining, though, can be infinitely worse. There's always someone who says, "Poor you! I fall asleep the minute my head hits the pillow."

Shut up! Shut up! Shut up!

Goldie's Legacy

EVERYTHING I UNDERSTAND about philanthropy, I learned from my great-auntie Goldie. The spirited youngest sister of my western Canadian grandmother was my gold standard of altruism.

I got to know my great-aunt after I joined the CBC in Winnipeg, where she lived. On my days off from work, we would take drives out of town or, since Goldie loved to eat, enjoy her favourite rib joint together. We regularly visited our dear departed relatives, including Goldie's mother, my great-grandmother. They were all buried in the Jewish cemetery not far from where she lived. We might stop to grab a few groceries on the way home, but this was always embarrassing for me. Goldie had to inform everyone in the store that her young great-niece appeared on television every night.

Like her eldest sister, Becky, my grandmother, Goldie was widowed early. But unlike my grandfather, who died solvent at fifty-nine, Goldie's husband left behind a mountain of debt. She had to work well into her sixties to clear it all. My grandmother's three professional sons and her daughter looked after their mother very well, especially after relocating her from Winnipeg to a nice apartment in Toronto. (Not that my grandma Pascoe ever expressed much gratitude for that. The two sisters could not have been more different in that regard.) Goldie had only one child, a daughter, who tragically died in her forties from cancer. Luckily, Goldie's three grandchildren lived close by, but her grandson, born with a disability, gave her a lot of worry.

Yet I never heard Goldie complain about anything. No one would suspect that she carried around so much heartache. She met the world with kindness, curiosity, and a twinkle in her eye. I admired her resilience as much as I loved her.

Goldie lived alone in a small basement studio apartment in the north end of Winnipeg, in a neighbourhood once home to many Jewish immigrants. After she retired, her only source of income was a monthly social security cheque. God forbid, though, she would ever be caught without ample supplies of poppy-seed cookies or apple strudel (tins of both were kept on the windowsill in the bathroom). Most weeks, she delivered her mouth-watering goodies to patients and staff at St. Boniface Hospital, where she'd had a pacemaker installed. I heard often how grateful she was to the doctors and nurses for saving her life. Goldie firmly believed in giving back. She did so with joy and baked goods.

Her tight financial circumstances became a sore point between my father and me. I was outraged that he didn't do more to help his auntie and didn't hesitate to tell him. Impatient with his inaction, one day I showed up at her door carrying a brand new colour television. Goldie loved to watch hockey, and I knew she would enjoy the set for games. I installed it, took away the ancient black-and-white one, and sent my father the bill. To his credit, he paid it promptly.

Many people donate to hospitals and other causes that matter to them. But do the gestures come with any sacrifice to their personal lifestyle? Rarely. I certainly didn't give up anything to buy that colour television. Goldie's tiny pension didn't leave much extra to spend at the grocery store, so in order to bake, she had to give up something else. That's what made her a true philanthropist. I learned a priceless lesson in selfless generosity from my dear auntie Goldie. I still miss her.

· · ·

I don't attend services at a synagogue on a regular basis, not even on the High Holidays. I stopped being observant as a teenager. I didn't want to worship a God who had taken my mother from me at such a young age, making me question His existence. The sound of the Jewish liturgy elevates many worshippers. When I hear it, though, I return to the day of my mother's funeral. The cantor's mournful voice made me cry harder than ever, well aware that all eyes in the crowded sanctuary of our synagogue were on our family.

I married Rodney, a Gentile. But I always considered myself Jewish, and I ended up embracing the teachings of Judaism that resonated with me, those that relate to charitable giving and community service in particular. These values prepared me well for the life I wanted to lead.

Of particular importance to me is *tzedakah*, a Hebrew word and tradition that translates as "righteous behaviour." In the modern world, it's a blanket term for philanthropy and charity and is considered an act of social justice. Donors feel they are sharing in God's work. The highest form of *tzedakah* is helping someone else to become self-sufficient.

Anonymity also figures prominently in the rules of *tzedakah*. I focused on that for years, preferring to fly under the radar with my donations, telling no one about them if I could help it. My mother's mother, Rose, famously told all her grandchildren never to draw attention to themselves. I took that sentiment to heart, unless I was trying to sell books. It was only after learning about the importance of leverage in fundraising that I decided to go public and throw off my cloak of anonymity. Leverage means inspiring others to give by showing people that you yourself have donated.

Learning to be transparent about my philanthropy took me hours of therapy. That sounds like a scene from a bad television drama, I know. What could possibly be difficult about coming into a lot of money? But after Rodney and I received our first big cheque from the sale of Maple Bear Latin America in 2016, I was a mess. We had not planned to say anything to our families about our windfall. Without us telling them, I figured no one would guess. We didn't move house, buy new cars, or engage in other visible signs of new wealth. But once the news was on the internet, after being leaked by the Brazilian press, we spilled the beans to those closest to us.

Rodney disagreed with my initial idea of giving away all the money immediately. "Why are you feeling so guilty about it?" he would ask. It wasn't like we'd won the lottery, he pointed out. He was right, of course. We had worked our asses off building Maple Bear, and we took a huge financial risk when we were in our fifties by betting our house on it. If our great risk hadn't worked out, we would be living a very different retirement right now.

Besides, Rodney had other ideas about how we could use the proceeds of our sale. He had learned by osmosis the other Jewish tradition that guided me: *tikkun olam*, which translates as "repairing the world." Judaism teaches that human beings are responsible for completing God's creation and improving the world. Under Rodney's direction, we took that message to heart by stepping up our commitment to environmental philanthropy, increasing our support for a wide range of groups taking climate action. We also provided the seed money for the start-up of Finca Cántaros, our daughter's environmental education not-for-profit in San Vito, Costa Rica.

I came up with the idea for a corporate philanthropy program that was perfect for Maple Bear as well. We would give our school owners, teachers, students, and families the opportunity to raise money for cancer research and, in the process, honour the legacy of Canadian hero Terry Fox. My eyes still well up whenever I see a picture of Terry. Like many Canadians of a certain age, I remember exactly where I was the day he was forced to end his gruelling Marathon of Hope for cancer research. It was the first day of September 1980, and I was in Winnipeg, 700 kilometres due west from Thunder Bay. That's where his incredible attempt to run right across Canada, on one leg, came to a screeching halt after 5,373 kilometres and the equivalent of a marathon a day for 143 straight days. The cancer that had claimed his leg had moved into his lungs. He had to stop.

For me and other staffers at the CBC, most of that day was spent staring at a television monitor. Numb and teary-eyed, none of us quite knew what to do or say. We could only watch as Terry, flanked by his parents, gave a final news conference before being carried to an ambulance on a stretcher. If things had turned out differently, Winnipeggers would have greeted him with a huge Prairie welcome along Portage Avenue. Canadians from coast to coast were shocked and heartbroken at the ending to this improbable fairy tale. Terry's story would go on to inspire multiple generations of schoolchildren in Canada and around the world.

Flash-forward almost forty years to 2018, to an entrance worthy of a visiting rock star. Several hundred boisterous students stamped their feet and cheered the arrival of their special guest, Terry's younger brother Darrell Fox. A school gymnasium thundered with the sound of their enthusiasm. As a student band stoically played on, an ordinary-looking middle-aged man charged through an impromptu receiving line. The huge welcome visibly surprised him, but he joyously accepted high-fives from the exuberant young crowd. Through his work with the Terry Fox Foundation, created soon after his brother's death in 1981, Darrell had met children from all over the world. That day, he was in Brazil, and the lively welcome came from students at the Maple Bear Canadian school in the country's capital city, Brasilia.

Once Darrell took his seat, all eyes, including those of Rick Savone, the Canadian ambassador to Brazil, shifted to a makeshift stage. Year 5 students were presenting their own abridged version of Terry's Marathon of Hope. It was a passionate performance, and particularly impressive for its delivery in flawless English, their second language after Portuguese. Like their hero had done, the students had pledged to raise one Canadian dollar for cancer research from each of their fellow classmates. The school's director announced that over five thousand dollars had been raised, mostly through sales of a T-shirt the students had designed. The money would support research at a national cancer hospital in São Paulo. Clad in one of those T-shirts, Rodney grabbed the microphone to announce that we would match their donation.

It had been easy to create a community investment program called The Joy of Giving Back and put Terry at the heart of it. Who better to embody the Canadian ideals Maple Bear wanted to foster in its students? Our brand declared we were educating the future leaders and citizens of a globalized world. Important values such as empathy, generosity, humility, resilience, and compassion were embodied in Terry's story, even four decades after his death. Moreover, cancer doesn't respect borders, making research into a cure a universal cause.

The Terry Fox Foundation has received well over half a million dollars from our program since we introduced Terry to our global family. We can thank my auntie Goldie for that.

A Road Not Taken

WE RARELY GET a glimpse during our time on earth of the roads not taken, of lives unlived. I was given that opportunity once, under heartbreaking circumstances: the funeral of my very first friend in the world. My beloved cousin Joey had lost her horrendous ten-year battle with metastatic brain cancer. She had defied the odds through numerous clinical drug trials. Every time we thought she was nearing the end, she would rally again. She simply would not give up.

As little girls, Joey and I were inseparable. Our mothers were sisters-in-law, Maritimers who had married two brothers from Western Canada. Though unrelated by blood, Bessie and Eve were connected through a labyrinth of Jewish family connections in Cape Breton, where both of them had grown up. As was the fashion in the 1950s among families, Joey and I lived around the corner from each other in a North Toronto neighbourhood. We were thrown together as soon as we could climb out of our cribs. Dragged around the city on their errands, we would regularly get separated from our mothers, only to be reunited after a grocery-store employee pronounced over the public address system, "If the mothers of Joanne and Robin Pascoe are still in the store, please come get them." Our parents socialized together, so Saturday night sleepovers were a regular thing, as were our respective birthday parties. Those later became annual phone calls.

Joey grew up to be a strikingly beautiful brunette. Her dark-brown eyes had an exotic olive shape. I would often tell her, to her delight, that she looked like the British actress Jane Seymour. As children, out and about with our mothers, Joey looked as if she belonged to mine. The resemblance between aunt and niece was striking. Being close to her aunt Bessie, my cousin always enjoyed the case of mistaken identity. On the night my mother died, Joey and I sobbed together.

When Joey died in 2019, mere months before the pandemic began, I almost didn't go to her funeral. I had already crossed the country twice that year to visit her, the last time barely two months before her death. To be honest, I was hoping to be out of the country, travelling on business, when the cancer finally took her. I wasn't sure I could face the finality of the ritual. But Rodney convinced me to fly to Toronto so I could attend her funeral.

I didn't learn anything new listening to the eulogies. I already knew my cousin was the beating heart of a huge extended community of family and friends. I had watched them surround her with so much love during her long illness. Joey didn't live in the spotlight. She left that to her glamorous older sister Lynda, whom she adored. As a devoted wife, loving mother, and tireless volunteer, my cousin led a full, rich life, even during the decade in which cancer slowly stole her life.

•   •   •

I was a pallbearer at her funeral. Her husband, Michael, told me my cousin would have wanted me to have that honour. I would have agreed to anything Michael asked: his extraordinary, loving care had been witnessed with a mixture of awe and jealousy by Joey's friends, who wondered how their own partners would deal with a wife's debilitating illness.

On that cold, crisp November day, I was one of eight mourners clinging to Joey's heavy coffin. We stood over her freshly dug grave, a freak snow squall clouding what had been a clear blue sky on the long drive up to the cemetery. *How does this hellish moment of watching you be laid to rest possibly qualify as an honour, Joey?*

But paying tribute to my cousin's life did allow me to marvel at how differently our lives had turned out after a shared golden childhood of toddler tea parties, sleepovers, Chanukah parties, and sleep-away summer camps. I was given that rare gift of a view of what might have been for me.

My cousin had followed a traditional path, marrying a nice Jewish boy and raising a loving family in Toronto. It might have been the path I had chosen if my mother hadn't died young, introducing a stepmother into my life and making Toronto the last place on earth I was ever going to call home. Joey's life ingrained her so deeply in her community that her death left a gaping hole in many people's daily lives. I travelled widely and chose to live far from my roots. Some might say I ran away from them, which wouldn't be far from the truth. On one important matter, though, Joey and I were aligned: we had both married Winnipeggers, choosing Prairie boys like our fathers, giving both of us long, happy marriages.

· · ·

The last time I spoke to Joey, it was from a Brazilian hotel room. Rodney and I were attending an annual Maple Bear convention for our school owners. It was also my birthday. As my beloved cousin and I chatted, I noticed that someone had apparently let themselves into our room while I was in the shower to drop off some convention swag. Joey couldn't believe that I was taking this invasion in stride, even laughing about it.

"How do you do it, Rob?" she asked me for the umpteenth time, neither of us knowing it would be the last one. "How do you handle all the crazy travel you do?"

I never got the chance to tell her that I could not have done it without her help. Joey was my North Star as she fought her cancer that decade. Whenever I started complaining about a late-night arrival in Nairobi or an endless security line in Dubai, I would ground myself by thinking about her, and how she never lamented the unfairness of her cancer and never gave up on living.

I saw so much of Bessie in Joey. It went beyond their physical resemblance. They were self-effacing, modest women, never deliberately drawing attention to themselves but attracting it nonetheless. Their funerals, more than fifty years apart, seemed eerily similar to me. Crowded sanctuaries for both of them, the air heavy with grief on a November day, the soulful, poignant sounds of the Hebrew mourners' Kaddish, the distraught family and friends. One day, I can only hope to be missed so much by so many.

Smug Idiots on a Coronavirus World Tour

A SINGLE UNIFORMED Sikh sentry stood guard at the main door into the Indira Gandhi International Airport in Delhi. His bland military headgear contrasted sharply with the brightly coloured turbans and saris worn by the crush of passengers inching their way towards him. Very slowly, or so it seemed to those waiting beside their overloaded luggage trolleys, he inspected passports and demanded proof of travel. The guard's real job, though, might have been to annoy the president and CEO of Maple Bear Global Schools.

Normally on our travel days, it was me grating on Rodney's nerves. That was usually in my role as wife, not as vice-president of corporate communications and social impact. At my anxious insistence, we had checked out of our hotel way too early, and he was still annoyed with me for that. Worse, I had tuned out his warnings over breakfast and consumed that second cup of *masala chai*. The long drive in congested Delhi traffic left me squirming with discomfort. I worried I might wet my pants if we didn't get inside the airport soon. When we finally made it to the entrance, the guard barely looked at our documents. Instead, he demanded the name of our airline, the departure time, even our assigned seat numbers—all noted on our boarding passes.

But that wasn't sufficient to confirm we were scheduled to get the hell out of India that day. Apparently, the gate number was missing.

"Turn around, man!" Rodney barked at him, indicating the glass entrance door. "You can see the board right behind you. There's our flight to Kathmandu. With the gate number. Now please let us in." With a grunt, the overzealous sentry stepped aside.

Rodney mumbled a thank-you, knowing he had acted badly. That was too often the way for foreigners travelling in India: you could hold it together for only so long before you cracked, and then struggled to find your manners again. In India, no action is ever simple. Or linear. Or involving just one person. That means, owing to frustration, you can end up acting like a jerk and creating a scene. Rodney had made a terrible fuss a day earlier at our hotel. Another guest had accidentally been shown into our room after midnight, awakening Rodney from a dead sleep and scaring the crap out of me as I lay awake praying to the sleep gods. The horrific, polluted Delhi air, seeping into the hotel's atrium every time the main front doors opened, had confused an employee escorting the late arrival: the room numbers were hard to read through the haze. The next morning, Rodney tore a strip off the poor front desk clerk. When we returned from meetings late in the afternoon, a chocolate cake was waiting in our room. *Sorry* had been iced on it. *Uh-oh.*

• • •

It was January 2020, a year now etched in global memory. Rodney and I were on a nine-country, fifteen-day journey, and Delhi was our sixth stop. We were sharing with our joint venture part-ners, in person, the news that we had sold the majority stake in Maple Bear to our Brazilian partners. After barely catching our breath in Casablanca, Bucharest, Istanbul, Dubai, and Muscat, Oman, we were departing India that day for Nepal. From Kath-mandu, we would go to Bangkok and finish up with a meeting in the Hong Kong airport. Our Hong Kong partner would arrive wearing a medical face mask, the first one we had seen on our trip. We even teased him about wearing it.

The coronavirus had been chasing us since the day we left Canada, but we ignored it. Even after dropping from our origi-nal itinerary countries like Vietnam (one of the first to close its borders), we were still in denial that the crisis could impact us. Our son, Jay, who worked with us, had a different opinion, and he urged us to start taking the situation seriously. Other family and friends sent concerned e-mails and links to news about the spread of the virus. In return, we shared pictures on social media of the Delhi pollution, proof in our minds that we would die of other stuff long before a virus could kill us. In other words, we were smug idiots.

• • •

Flights still hadn't been grounded when our tour picked up again in mid-February. We had barely unpacked in Vancouver before returning to the airport, this time armed with disin-fectant wipes and hand sanitizer (but not masks) and heading for São Paulo, Brazil. The new majority owners were planning to make an announcement to school owners and the press. It was the second time we had made a deal with one of Brazil's biggest education conglomerates, which had global aspirations. Unprecedented economic growth in that country, combined with an emerging middle class, had put us on their radar. With hundreds of schools spread out across the vast South American nation, Brazil remains the jewel in the Maple Bear crown.

Contrary to what shows like *Succession* may portray, the negotiations for our first sale had been incredibly low-key. About a dozen of us camped out for two long days in the fall of 2016 in a meeting room in the basement of a four-star hotel in Los Gatos, California. With neither windows nor clocks, it could have been Vegas without the slots. Pizzas were brought in for lunch, and we travelled in Ubers, not limos. The sixty-something Brazilian CEO wore a hoodie and spoke very little English, handing the deal-making over to his English-speaking daughter, who was younger than our own. The scene was so utterly lacking in the television trappings of great wealth that we could almost have forgotten who we were dealing with. The reality was hammered home a few months later, when we flew to their hometown of Ribeirão Preto on the family's corporate jet. After we announced our second deal, and with the pandemic looming larger in February 2020, I would have been thrilled if that jet could have flown us back to Canada. No such luck. (That second agreement, at least, had been hammered out in Vancouver months earlier.)

• • •

Idiots that we were, we ignored world events well into the early weeks of March 2020. Barely back from negotiating and deal-making, we travelled to Costa Rica to see our daughter, Lilly. While we were there, the World Health Organization made the announcement that stopped the world, and we caught the first plane back to Canada. Six weeks had passed since our sale officially closed and the money was securely in the bank. But as the pandemic spread around the globe, Maple Bear schools too began to close. The smug idiots smartened up at last, diving into crisis management on behalf of the thousands of people who had trusted us and now depended on our leadership.

It would be eighteen months before we boarded a plane again. This time, we did so for personal reasons. During the pandemic, Lilly created the Finca Cántaros Environmental Association, in San Vito, Costa Rica. The not-for-profit environmental education centre takes its name from the existing tourist property of 7.5 hectares and adjacent pastureland that we helped her purchase in 2018. It had long been a professional goal of Lilly's to have an environmental project that she could lead. Our daughter also delivered on another dream of hers (and ours too) by bringing into the world our first grandchild, Lucy Rose Rodríguez Briggs.

San Vito is far off the regular tourist path in a scenic mountainous, rural corner of the southern zone of the country, not far from Panama. Costa Rica is known as the "Green Republic" for its commitment to environmental initiatives, so Finca Cántaros joined a number of organizations and researchers already working, some for many decades, in the biodiverse Central American nation.

Besides Lilly's "baby," Finca Cántaros has also become a family project for us, one that is quickly putting down roots, both literally and metaphorically. Lilly and her team, including Lucy's father, David, a biologist, photographer, and top birding guide in

Costa Rica, are passionate about nurturing environmental stewardship in the local community. They are using forest restoration and birds as educational tools. Every weekend, there's something going on: women are painting and composting together, families are on bird walks that even our granddaughter is enjoying, and students are planting trees and being invited to come back to watch and help them grow. There is so much more I could say about Finca Cántaros, but I will leave that for another time. As it is, I'm on a steep learning curve as her official advisor on fundraising communications (and video producer).

Rodney, too, has found his next calling—and his true legacy. When we are visiting San Vito, the former president and CEO of Maple Bear gladly exchanges his computer for a machete, building bird blinds, hiking trails, and a burgeoning not-for-profit start-up. If, in the future, Lilly's environmental education model is scaled up and established in other parts of the world, she has no better advisor than her father to help her. After all, working with our son, Jay (who now handles financial matters for his sister's organization), Rodney took an idea for a Canadian bilingual preschool program and founded Maple Bear, now in close to forty countries around the world, with over 550 schools.

In 2023, Lilly was interviewed by Cornell University's Civic Ecology Lab for a documentary about her work. She was asked what lessons she had received from her parents that have influenced her. Lilly didn't hesitate for a moment. She told the interviewer that it was her father, the nature lover, who took her out birding from a young age. "He was the one who opened my eyes to the magical world of birds," she said. "From my dad, I was really inspired to love and appreciate nature."

And from her mother? She said I provided logistical support so she could strategize ways to inspire her friends to not only appreciate nature but also to save it. (Her library still holds all the *How to Save the Planet* books I bought her as a child.) "My mom taught me how to channel my love of nature into positive social action," she said. My eyes well up just writing that. As a child, Lilly created an endless number of school activities around the environment, beginning when she was eight years old and attending the International School of Beijing. Together, we created an environmental Brownies troop, sending little girls running around the school stopping toilets from running too long and wasting water. It was the beginning of her career as an environmental educator.

While it had its challenges, Rodney's diplomatic career gave our children a unique childhood. Now, our daughter's lifelong passion for saving the planet has bestowed upon us a wonderful gift in retirement. We can't say we didn't see it coming.

Acknowledgements

I AM GRATEFUL to my many friends and relatives who supported me on my intense three-year journey of writing down all the stories that appear in this collection. I am especially grateful, however, to my editors, Barbara Pulling and Naomi Pauls. They, more than anyone else, helped me shape my life review into something not only readable but also a memoir that will hopefully resonate with others. I'm also grateful to the designer Jan Perrier for helping me navigate the multiple electronic versions now required and for creating the beautiful print edition and my website too. Janice Bearg, my publishing mentor who first encouraged me to self-publish my expat books over twenty years ago, was dragged into this process again, and she too kept me moving forward. And, of course, I must thank my long-suffering husband, Rodney, who had the misfortune of marrying this writer. I truly could not have finished this book without his love and support. He remains my biggest cheerleader.

About the Author

ROBIN PASCOE is the author of five books about global living. She has never been awarded a scholarship, a fellowship, an honorary degree, or a prize for her writing, her volunteerism, or her philanthropy. She did, however, win Best Girl Camper 1966 at Camp Kadimah, probably for her bubbly personality. At the age of sixty, after stepping back as the Expat Expert, Pascoe joined her husband and son to create a brand for their family's wildly successful global education company, Maple Bear. Now, in her so-called retirement, she is helping out with another family project, fighting climate change in rural Costa Rica at an environmental education not-for-profit founded by her daughter. She currently divides her time between two paradises: magical Costa Rica and beautiful British Columbia, Canada.

Robin's Books for Expatriate Families

"With her unique combination of warmth, understanding, humour, and feisty advocacy, Robin Pascoe has become a beloved standard-bearer for women accompanying their partners on overseas assignments. I'm very glad that *A Broad Abroad* will continue to guide and reassure new generations of expat women. This honest and supportive book was, and is, a landmark contribution to the cause."

—**PATRICIA LINDERMAN,** author of *The Expert Expat*

"Out of years of personal experience and interaction with other expatriates and Third Culture families, Robin Pascoe has caught the essence of the challenges and struggles that all too often are faced by internationally mobile people without the appropriate and proper warnings. *Homeward Bound* is a book written from both the head and the heart, and it speaks to the head and the heart of the reader."

—**DAVID POLLOCK,** co-author, *Third Culture Kids: Growing Up Among Worlds*

"Robin may have written *A Moveable Marriage* for spouses struggling to find their old—or new—identity before, during, and after a relocation, but it's good, solid, and helpful reading for anyone whose marriage has lost some luster and needs to shine again."

—**FRANCESCA KELLY,** retired US State Department spouse

"*Raising Global Nomads* is about change, what lies ahead, how to prepare for it, and how to deal with it. I particularly enjoyed the chapter about transforming global nomads into global citizens. After all, our children really want to make a difference in the world!"

—**SANDY THOMAS,** former director, USA Girl Scouts Overseas

Printed in the USA
CPSIA information can be obtained
at www.ICGtesting.com
LVHW061649260224
772870LV00062B/2164